No Way Out But Through

A Songwriter's Slow, Blind Journey from Chaos to Clarity

KENT MAXSON
with DAVID TEEMS

Fitting Words
Nashville, Tennessee

"Kent is a wonderful writer indeed—with all the skills you'd expect from a Nashville pro. But what makes his writing so special is his great big heart. Every word comes straight from there!"

"I love that guy! Every song from Kent is filled with a crystal-clear vision of the emotion it is written to evoke."

"This book is a must-read for everyone who has walked through pain and suffering, desperately trying to hang onto the promises of God. Through the power of song Kent tears open the curtain and reveals his personal story of pain, faith, and transformation."

Publishing services provided by Fitting Words, LLC—Nashville, TN.
To contact the publisher, visit: www.fittingwords.net.

Cover design by Man of War Creative Studios.
To contact the designer, visit: www.manofwarcreative.com.

The poem "A Servant to Servants" by Robert Frost (source for title) is in the public domain.

Quotes from the following published works of David Teems used with permission:
The Myst of Eden Series: More Hope, Budding Grove Audio, © 1996.
To Love Is Christ, Thomas Nelson/Harper Collins, © 2005.
And Thereby Hangs a Tale, Harvest House, © 2010.

Print ISBN: 979-8-9871314-9-7
All Scriptures is taken from the English Standard Version of the Bible unless otherwise noted. Abbreviations for Bible versions used:

GNT	Good News Translation
KJV	King James Bible
MSG	The Message
NASB1995	New American Standard Bible 1995
NCV	New Century Version

NIV   New International Version
NKJV   New King James Bible
NLT   New Living Translation

For my dad, Rodney Maxson

If you wish to purchase a CD or a digital download of the songs and music videos referenced in this book, scan the QR code on the last page.

You may also visit Kent's web site at: www.kentmaxson.com.

Contents

Acknowledgments

Each of the songs included in this project was co-written with one or two other gifted songwriters. For me to take credit without sharing the spotlight would not be right. So, to the audio engineers, musicians, and my fellow songwriters who helped me to create the musical moments in this project, I want to express my heartfelt thanks. Adam James Deiboldt, Randy Finchum, Michael Jarrett, Matt Wynn, JK Nick Nichols, David MacKechnie, Jordan Mogey, Buddy Mondlock, Marc Roberts, Carl Saff, Cody Smith and Alyssa Trahan, I cannot adequately express my gratitude for allowing me to be a part of creating meaningful songs with each of you. I want to thank the gifted Barbara Potter for the excellent photography for this project (Barbara Potter Photography).

I discovered early in this project that writing songs and writing a book are two very different things. I want to thank my good friend, best-selling author, David Teems, who supplied the necessary language and structure for things I struggled to say, setting them to a kind of music of their own. Supplying many of his own concepts to complement mine added depth to this manuscript I could not have anticipated. For these things I am forever grateful.

May all that has been reduced to noise in you become music again.

David Teems, *To Love Is Christ*

Introduction
Underneath the Noise

Country Music Hall of Fame songwriter Harlan Howard once said, "Country music ain't nothin' but three chords and the truth." That just means a song is some happy fusion of downhome simplicity and character, of farsightedness and charm, that you don't need four chords or five when three will work just fine. While I could not agree more with Mr. Howard's assessment, master craftsman that he was, and while I have done my best to live by that motto, he knew there was much more to it than that. What Harlan Howard knew, what all songwriters know, is that a song is able to say things that other forms of communication most often can't, that a song engages the imagination and emotions like no other form of expression, and that under the influence of imaginative language, it is able to reach parts of us that are often hidden away or remote—those things we keep to ourselves, the deep and tender parts. It is the latter, those deep and tender parts, that this book is about.

Because human interaction can be messy at times, and often with those closest to us, there will always be things that need to be said, things that at times only a lyric or a poem can say or dare to say, language with the necessary reach and penetration. Every songwriter knows that. He or she also knows timing and word choice are critical. Songwriting is an unusual calling, and every songwriter comes to it in his or her own way. Me? I was wounded into it. But hold that thought for the moment.

When creating a thing of beauty or fascination, whether writing a song, authoring a book, painting, sculpting, writing an essay or a poem—it hardly matters—the creative act will follow a similar pattern whatever the medium, a process that is, literally, older than time.

> Now the earth was formless and empty, darkness was over the surface of the deep, and the Spirit of God was hovering over the waters. And God said, "Let there be light," and there was light.
>
> **Genesis 1:2–3**

First, there is a lack of order, blankness, a chaos of a particular kind. Every song idea, every image, every inspired moment that hopes to become a work of art, however grand or however humble, is without shape or substance—that is, undiscovered. For a song to emerge from this stew will demand trial after trial, experiment upon experiment, some hits, some misses—looking under every metaphorical rock, through every chink—auditioning one phrase, one line, then another, against a melody that may itself be unshaped. It may mean trashing an idea altogether and starting over. The point is the songwriter willingly enters this riot of creation, and while it may not be the most comfortable place to be, he or she knows that is where the music is, that success means emerging *from* this chaos, and with a song. It implies a pioneering of self, so to speak. If this part of the process is unavoidable, and it is, it is also necessary, stretching the songwriter, as it does, beyond former imaginative limits, all in the attempt to discover the poetry underneath the noise, the beauty hiding in the dark. I am talking about songwriting, of course, but this process offers a useful image of growth and forward movement in matters of the spirit.

When my own life began to drift (or plunge) into disorder and chaos, all I wanted to do was "emerge," that is, to get to the other side. I found out quickly, however, that I could not tiptoe around it, detour, skip a step, negotiate with God, promise to be a good boy, or close my eyes hoping it would go away. I had no choice but to walk through it (sometimes stumble, sometimes crawl), formless and empty as it was—as I was—without light or roadmap. I certainly didn't think of my life as a potential work of art, that this emptiness had purpose or any bearing at all on who I was or what I was to become. I can say now it was worth it, that I had to endure the worst that I might know God's truest and best.

When the light came on at last, I was altered. Sure, there will always be refinements to consider, the "from glory to glory" kind, but I was whole again. There was meaning in all I suffered, and beauty. God was the songwriter. I was the song. Like creation itself in its slow, blind journey from chaos to clarity, to borrow a line from a Robert Frost poem, there was "no way out but through."

While each chapter in this book will include a song lyric and a chapter to go with it, the point is not the song itself—how I wrote it, who I pitched it to, who recorded it, or any of those things. A well-written song needs no explanation but itself, which is the very thing we love about it. It leaves us satisfied and craving more at the same time. Kind of like love. Or the spiritual life. As suggested above, a song has a hidden life of its own. And while a lyric may not seem to tell all, it says just enough to make you feel something deeply and get a sense of meaning that goes beyond explanation. While songwriting plays a part in this book, if but a metaphorical one (an image of creation), this book is not about a song. It is about a songwriter—me. It is the account of one man's acquisition of spiritual backbone and the costs involved in its purchase.

The idea of putting a song and a book together isn't all that new. King Solomon once said, "What has been will be again, what has been done will be done again; there is nothing new under the sun" (Ecclesiastes 1:9, NIV). While lines like that seem to take the fun right out of everything, especially if you are a creative thinker striving for originality, Solomon is worth taking a brief look.

Solomon was a songwriter, a remarkable one considering his many responsibilities as king. And with 700 wives and 300 concubines, it's a wonder he had time to write much of anything. Forgive the levity, but songwriting came naturally to Solomon. It was in his blood. Hank Williams Jr. might say it was a "family tradition." Solomon's dad was a songwriter. King David not only wrote songs and lots of them, he played guitar as well, or at least some early form of one. Like Hank Sr., King David was more troubled than his son, a little more famous, his reputation a little darker, his agony more agonized, his struggles deeper and more penetrating, his songs more memorable. Most of them came at an unspeakable cost. Because of that, Dad's songs have a different tone than those of his son, a different music (again, not unlike the Hanks), sung best in a minor key. But when his songs celebrate, there is no splendor like them, no greater height that words can reach. Warrior poet that he was, David gave words to joy and despair the way only a poet of the highest order could, writing some of the most beautiful lines ever written, the kind we love to commit to memory, that we love to speak out loud.

> The LORD is my shepherd; I shall not want.
> He maketh me to lie down in green pastures.

> **Psalm 23:1–2, KJV**

The LORD is my light and my salvation—whom shall I fear?
The LORD is the stronghold of my life—of whom shall I be afraid?

Psalm 27:12, NIV

Where can I go from your Spirit? Where can I flee from your presence? If I go up to the heavens, you are there; if I make my bed in the depths, you are there. If I rise on the wings of the dawn, if I settle on the far side of the sea, even there your hand will guide me, your right hand will hold me fast.

Psalm 139:7–10, NIV

Unlike his father, Solomon wrote one long and delicious love song—symphonic, ecstatic, oozing with honey or myrrh. In its way, you could say it is a book of songs, with titles like "More Delightful Than Wine," "Your Name Is Like Perfume," "Until the Day Breaks and the Shadows Flee," "Among the Lilies," "His Banner Over Me Is Love," "A Love as Strong as Death," and many more. It is one of the most beautiful books in the Bible, if not in all world literature, and it is found in the very heart of Scripture, in its warm center, a steamy little number called Song of Solomon. Both a song and a book, it exposes the romance of God and in an English language worthy of it. The following excerpt demonstrates the deathless resilience of love.

Set me as a seal upon thine heart, as a seal upon thine arm: for love is as strong as death; jealousy is cruel as the grave: the coals thereof are coals of fire, which hath a most vehement flame. Many waters cannot quench love, neither can floods drown it: if a man would give all the substance of his house, it would utterly be contemned.

Song of Solomon, 8:6–7, KJV

Of the many things songwriting demands of a writer, a refined sense of organization is one of the more necessary ones—each word in its place, each phrase, each verse, all contributing to the architecture and beauty of a single piece of music. Solomon, whose reputation for wisdom was already widely known, was therefore entrusted by God to build his house (temple) in Jerusalem, an honor that his father, David, a man of blood, was denied. It was a house of worship. The plans were specific. There were to be three sections, or courts, each one separated from the other by a curtain. The first curtain was at the gate of the outer courtyard that separated the people from the tabernacle. The second curtain separated the outer courtyard from the Holy Place. Only priests were allowed to enter the Holy Place. The third curtain opened the way into the Most Holy Place, otherwise known as the Holy of Holies. The high priest alone could enter the Holy of Holies, and only once a year on the Day of Atonement. On that day, he would make a blood offering to God. The offering was placed on the mercy seat as an atonement offering for his sins and the sins of the people. It was this third curtain, the one that allowed entrance into the Most Holy Place, that was torn in two at the death of Jesus.

And when Jesus had cried out again in a loud voice, he gave up his spirit. At that moment the curtain of the temple was torn in two from top to bottom. The earth shook, the rocks split.

Matthew 27:50–52, NIV

. . . where our forerunner, Jesus, has entered on our behalf. He has become a high priest forever, in the order of Melchizedek.

Hebrews 6:20, NIV

Not to twist us up in a metaphor, but this tear in the fabric simply means that the way to God is open. We no longer have to put on fancy robes, endure long and lavish ceremonies, kill a goat, a lamb, or any other creature, or go behind any curtain with some secret language to approach God. Christ provided a simpler and more efficient way. The way is costly, certainly, but it is a way of freedom, the purest kind of freedom found only in Christ, our high priest, who lives among us and who abides sweetly in our hearts. We do not have to use church language or special songs to communicate, praise, or worship God. We can approach him as we are—with what words we have or with that which has no words. This allows us access not only to God, but to that innermost chamber of ourselves, having removed the partition that separates me from me, ourselves from ourselves, the deeper knowledge of which, while costly, allows you and me to deal more efficiently with those pesky emotional and psychological woes that burden us, those strongholds that cheat us of the power to change.

As redemption does its mysterious work, I not only have deeper and truer access to myself, to my inner court, it rends the veil between myself and others as well. Is it easy? Or painless? Not exactly.

AFTER THE FIRE

I am a Nashville songwriter. I have had my share of successes, as many Nashville songwriters have. I have a gold record on my wall. Songwriting is what I was put upon this earth to do. Did I come by that revelation early? In some ways I did. When you grow up in a household of creative folks and want your moment in the sun, you tend to discover early what you do best. I was fortunate that way. Writing songs helped me work out some issues of my own and make music out of them. Still, the part you're not told as a kid (or if you are told, you don't have the tools to understand) is that certain conditions have to be met first, and most of them I was not prepared for.

Truth is, I was prepared for very little. Though I knew I wanted to be a songwriter, it took years to become a reality. My journey to the craft was a long one. I had to experience a whole lot of life before any song would dare entrust itself to my keeping. It is not a matter of pounce and grab. That's not how it works. Because a song (or a book) is a living thing, it becomes a partnership of a kind. You could call it a courtship under a certain light. I have suffered for my understanding. But the end was and remains not only worth it, but there was also much music in it. "After the fire," Scripture says, came a still small voice. I tremble to think about it now. Only then, only after life has left a few indelible prints, do you possibly have anything of value to say.

You often hear songwriters say of a song that "it wrote itself," meaning simply that the song was easy in them, that they did the work of listening first, listening deeply, that by some instinct they knew when to be aggressive and when not to, when to push, when to wait. It is a beautiful process, not unlike falling in love. There is a law of attraction at work. An idea or a story that becomes a song will demand words that not only stick but that have the movement, those musical qualities and power that make them irresistible and inevitable. All that to say, the best thing one can do for a song is to let it happen. Another way to say it, and this applies to the spiritual life as well, is to surrender to it, to the process. This takes years of learning the craft both on its surface and underneath (where there is always a lot going on), but the long apprenticeship is worth it.

The ability to communicate well, to write with polish and impact, to put words on paper or to a strain of music, can be used for good. It can also be used for purposes that are not so good. A well-written, well-thought-out text can deliver necessary insight at the very moment insight is needed. Or

No Way Out But Through

it can be used to distract, to hide sinister motives and evil intent. What that requires of me is responsible use of language. Why? Because it matters. Let me repeat that: Because it matters. Scripture says so.

Death and life are in the power of the tongue, and those who love it will eat its fruits.

Proverbs 18:21

Look at the ships also, though they are so great and are driven by strong winds, are still directed by a very small rudder wherever the inclination of the pilot desires. So also the tongue is a small part of the body, and yet it boasts of great things.

James 3:4–5, NASB1995

By way of stories and songs, I have done my best to express some of the experiences I have encountered in my life and how they have shaped my faith and bestowed on me the clarity I lacked, to be able to see and think and process as God has appointed. Feel free to test every word of every line in this book against the truth found in Scripture. That includes every song, whether you listen to it or read the lyric. Not every song I have included in this book is necessarily a "Christian" song, though underneath all of them lies the hope of Christ.

Like you, I have sought answers to countless questions about who Jesus is, grappling with my inner monologue, unsettling as it is at times, on how he can possibly forgive or love me. I am not a Bible scholar, nor am I an authority on the God I profess to follow. Not having written a book before, I had help with that too. Like many of you, I am a perpetual student, a sinner who has figuratively crawled to the foot of the cross looking for freedom and release from my own sins, and, ultimately, to know the quiet heart that comes with revelation of him who once hung there. Like you, I have been lost, found, unfound, found again, saved, punished, forgiven, hopeless, redeemed, crushed, reborn, ignored, and loved. And there is a lot of music in all that.

At last, Jesus said, "You will be my witnesses—in Jerusalem, in all of Judea, in Samaria, and in every part of the world" (Acts 1:8, NCV). I am not his salesperson or his defense attorney. He wants you and me to be his witness, to let the power of our words, the persuasion of the Holy Spirit, and the sacred text written within each of them to do its strange work, offering, as it does, revelation, redemption, and the liberty it invites and celebrates not only for you, reader, but for me as well. I just thought it time to put it down on paper.

Chapter 1
I Never Dreamed You'd Speak So Softly

If you've answered, Lord, I must have missed it.
Are you near, 'cause all I hear are crickets. . .

Kent Maxson and Randy Finchum, "Crickets"

How do you sustain your faith in God when life does not go as you planned, or when God doesn't show up as you were convinced he should? What are we to think when prayers seem ineffective and heaven mute? How can a person have faith in an all-loving God when after screaming out in pain there is only silence? I suppose there are answers for these questions, and I am certain none of them are easy. I know I didn't have any. Such things most often have to be woven into a song, a book, a sonnet, something.

Historically, art has always been the best outlet for the difficult questions of life, joy when it has no words, or heartbreak. Without a history or a philosophy lecture, art has a way of getting underneath such questions, of penetrating the very heart of them and finding a way in that might not have been thought of otherwise. For me, that choice was clear: I would write a song. Even so, I wrestled with the idea for years. And, as you might guess, it wrestled back. It would not leave me alone, nor would the questions that drove it, the ones that at last bullied me into words. I had no choice but to do the work, to sit down and write the lyric, to free myself of the troubling thing that empowered it.

In March of 2020, I finally put pen to paper and wrote the song with my good friend Randy Finchum. We called it "Crickets," inspired by that sound, or lack of sound you get from an audience when the joke doesn't work, your tale goes flat, or, in this case, when there is no one at the other end of your question. A form of prayer itself, I thought writing a song would be enough, that hacking out a thoughtful lyric might be sufficient to get the attention from heaven I so desperately wanted. I was wrong. I felt the joy any songwriter feels when he or she writes what they feel is a good song, but that wasn't the joy I was after. That is when I had the idea for this book.

A song or a poem has the advantage of elevated speech, figurative language, clever images to captivate a listener, the charm of rhyme and rhythm to give it movement, and ornamentation that might just weave three minutes into magic. A book can and often does have those same qualities, but by its sheer length and plainer speech, a book is able to explore, make discoveries, and sound depths a song cannot always go. It has the reach, substance, and power to inform in the way a song is limited. That is not to say that a song is something less. Hardly. To be fair, a song can touch the listener in ways a book cannot, to make emotional and intellectual pleas that don't always lend themselves to prose. To say that one sings and the other explains may be one way of looking at it, but that doesn't say enough, nor does it say it with complete accuracy. It hardly matters. The beauty of this book lies in the cooperation between the two. You, reader, have the advantage of both.

Whether writing a song or a book, each demands its own specific kind of labor. I have been writing songs for years and am comfortable with it, but to write what I hoped would become a book took some getting used to. My idea was to write chapters to go with certain songs. Each time I tried to tell about the events that led me to write "Crickets," I ran into obstacles. So, I got help, someone with verbal skills and a good ear, who has written books before. When I did, words came at last.

I pray this book does justice to the events I am about to explain: events that altered me, that altered my entire life, that shook me to my roots, and that ultimately set me on another course—one truer to the path Christ prepared for me. It was like a perfect storm of events when not just one bad (and unexpected) thing happened, but another, then another, then another, and so on, a Category 5 wind capable of uprooting everything. To be clear, this book is not an explanation of a few songs as much as it is an exploration of those events that, in time, could only be written in a song.

Because of its brevity, a song doesn't ask for or even need absolute clarity. It uses metaphor instead, figurative speech that makes the point and doesn't have to use specific language to explain. For instance, when we read or hear the word *cross* in a Christian context, we know it represents one of the most cruel and brutal punishments man could ever devise. Therefore, the use of the word alone is sufficient. The gruesome detail is implied but not always necessary to say. But while a book will use the occasional figurative language, it can tell the whole tale, including all woes, all successes and failures, and with as much detail as necessary for the author to say what he or she thinks needs to be said and with the appropriate language to say it. The Bible has songs, but it also provides a complete rendering of God's word—not too much or too little, but just enough. That is my hope for this book.

My story will not be complete without a few words about the divorce. I say that with the understanding that it is not fair to my girls or my ex-wife to repeat the tale or parts of it that changed all our lives. I hope they will forgive me. I hope they know me or know my heart well enough to know that mercy and forgiveness are the best things we can do for each other, that the long arm of redemption has the necessary reach, that my story is, in part, their story, and that it may prove with great hope that the truth indeed can make us free. "Above all," Scripture says, "love each other deeply, because love covers over a multitude of sins" (1 Peter 4:8, NIV). In my first marriage, my wife and I spent twenty out of the twenty-six years in some kind of marriage counseling. We tried for years to fix something that we both suspected was broken. We went through counseling, for one reason, because we thought it worth it. We had four children, four little girls who looked to us for love and sanctuary.

THE FALLOUT

I am a recovering worrier. If there is a way to become anxious about something, I will find it—or make something up if I have to. You know the kind. The human mind is surely capable of such self-sabotage. But not this time. I didn't make this up. Who could? Who would want to?

I have heard that the five most stressful things a person can go through in life are death of a loved one, a divorce, moving, major illness or injury, and job loss. Other than the death of a loved one, in 2013 I experienced all these events. The fallout was disastrous. In February, I was rushed to the emergency room with chest pains. The medical staff took one look at me and rushed me into the operating room. Before falling asleep, I squeezed in a few prayers, all of them immediate, close to the surface: I told my wife I loved her. I asked God to take care of my children. I asked him to heal me and to please let me wake up again. He may have been first in my thoughts, but there was more panic than confidence in those prayers. My religion, all the formalities and calm, ran for cover, so to speak. There were no *thees* and *thous*. I didn't call him *Heavenly Father*. All my assurances failed me. I had professed Jesus all my life, and now I was scared. The thought that I might not wake up from this awful dream was too much. "God, be with me" is all I could manage.

After so much time and so much talk, did I really believe him? There were serious reasons to panic. I can say now how grateful I was for that awareness, however frightening it was.

After waking from surgery, and after a brief moment of gratitude for being part of the world again, I asked the doctors what had happened. They told me I had pericarditis and atrial fibrillation. Over the next seven months, I suffered four more trips to the emergency room, each with a barrage of tests, scans, and procedures. The medical bills compounded the strain I already had from having a mortgage and two daughters in college. All this resulted in the doctors telling me I needed two heart ablation surgeries. The panic never subsided. It simply maintained a low profile. Still in control of my thought life, what choice did I have but to move forward?

In August, just before my first heart ablation surgery, my wife of twenty-six years told me she was thinking about divorcing me. I was in the fight of my life, only to get the wind knocked out of me by the one person I would have never suspected. Then, the weekend after the first surgery and just three weeks before my second one, my boss called to tell me the company I was working for was going out of business, that my last official day of employment (and insurance coverage) would be the day after my second surgery. His timing was as ill-charmed as my wife's.

My bills are bigger than the checks I'm getting,
The rumor is the shop will be shutting down.
Some days I feel like giving up and quitting.
I'm listening for your voice as I cry out,
"Where are you now?"

The loneliness I felt was unlike anything I had ever felt or was prepared to feel. Nor was it over. During the next three months, my wife and I went to a marriage counselor, but it was merely an exercise, one that had the appearance of hope but none of its substance. So, in spite of the counseling and all the prayers requested, on the morning of November 20, she told me she had made up her mind: She wanted a divorce. I moved out of our house that day.

Where was God in all this? The question burned in me. Or it should have. But I was already burned. In the rotten state I was in, Jesus could have stepped out of a cloud and I'm not sure I would have even noticed. I was a crash victim, still reeling, still trying to find my feet. The question haunted me, nonetheless, and at many levels—not all of them friendly—I could do little but stare at it. If there were answers, they were late.

The memory of the next forty-five days or so remains a blur. I was forced to live out of a suitcase, to impose on my friends for a place to stay while putting our house on the market—the house we had raised our children in, where we had lived for twenty-two years as husband and wife, as mother and father, a house I thought was more than a house, once a sanctuary, a home, the memories of which stung grievously, coming back to me as they did in small bursts of clarity, those meaningful and unforgettable moments when we were a family.

Often, in the middle of the night, I would wake up with panic attacks (that's all I knew to call them). *How? Why? When?* Again, there were no

No Way Out But Through

answers, and I was too overwhelmed to have recognized one had there been any, all my belongings now in the back of a rented truck.

I was a mess. I don't remember trying to decide where I wanted to live or what to do with the rest of my life. Life was reduced to putting one foot in front of the other without a compass, and certainly without a still small voice to guide or comfort me in this small hell I had stumbled into. I somehow knew I would return to Nashville. I don't know if it was a conscious decision or if something else had awakened in me—a calling I had ignored for twenty-two years. I will say more about that in a moment.

Steve Reiter, one of my best friends and basketball teammates in high school, flew in to help me move. On January 8, 2014, the two of us started our long drive to Nashville—me driving my new used car (another story, another song) and Steve driving the rented truck. I remember the odd sense of déjà vu I felt when I returned to Nashville. In the twenty-two years I had been gone, my former roommates, Kevin and Bob, had bought houses next door to each other. Kevin offered to let me stay with him until I got back on my feet. Bob got some of his employees to help me unload my belongings into storage. Thanks to their help, I had a place to live and a place to store my stuff.

I was a fifty-six-year-old man starting life over again with the same friends who had taken me in thirty years earlier. I was returning to the town I never wanted to leave in the first place. Leaving Nashville the first time had been a mistake, one I did not intend to make again.

I was waiting for my divorce to be final. I no longer owned a house. I had no job, and my residence was a rented bedroom with my life's memories stored in a garage. I went to bed that first night thinking, "I'm a failure. I haven't progressed at all in life." Hurt and lonely, I felt like God had abandoned me. In spite of the silence, I cried out again, "Where are you, God?"

RAGGED

There is really no way to explain the pain of divorce. Being an elder in my previous church, I remember visiting couples who were going through it, convinced that I understood their pain. After all, I had experienced break-ups with girlfriends in high school and college. "God has a plan," I would say. "All you need to do is trust him." It grieves me to think about that now. Not that God didn't have a plan or that trusting him would be wrong, but how could I have possibly understood their pain? It was only through suffering my own divorce that I began to know anything at all. Wisdom comes at a price.

When I moved to Nashville, I quickly learned that the night was not my friend. Distractions are easy to find during the day. But when you are by yourself at night, the loneliness can be overwhelming. If Scripture is true, and I believe it is, it suggests that a man and a woman become one flesh. Not one spirit, but one flesh. It seemed logical, therefore, that divorce is a kind of violence against that flesh, a kind of tearing apart. I had trouble sleeping. I would stay up all night, every night. When I did manage to sleep, I usually woke at three or four in the morning, my heart racing. I offered countless prayers to God.

I begged.

I pleaded.

I bargained.

I made countless promises.

I folded my hands.

I reached out with my arms towards the ceiling.

But try as I might, I felt like every word I said stopped at the ceiling and never made it beyond the bedroom.

'Cause all I hear are crickets

And the evening breeze blowing through the trees.

I send you prayers from on my knees,

Begging you, God, please talk to me.

If you've answered, Lord, I must have missed it.

Are you near? 'Cause all I hear are crickets.

Many times, I would put my warm-ups on and go for a walk in the dead of night. The winter air felt good against my face, and broken as I was, it was a nice change to feel something, anything. I wandered up and down the blacktop roads of a secluded neighborhood and usually ended up at the local high school track, where I could walk or run until I collapsed from fatigue. I would then make my way back along the dark streets to my bedroom in Kevin's house.

When there are no cars out, and you are walking in the darkness of the night, you hear things you might have missed otherwise. The barking of a dog makes a lonely sound—the hum of streetlights, a small critter scampering in the bushes, moonlight, and stars that kept me company. Walking in this area of Nashville felt like I was in the country, the night around me, nature (creation) talking to me, and me not having to talk back. It had a calming effect.

> Wait for the LORD; be strong, and let your heart take courage;
> wait for the LORD!
>
> **Psalm 27:14**

When you hurt, when you cry out to God, what would it take for you to believe he is listening, that he cares? What do you do when you call out and there is no reply, or at least nothing you can recognize? Does his apparent lack of response mean he does not exist or doesn't care? Even Jesus experienced the silence of God. He, too, cried out.

> And at the ninth hour Jesus cried with a loud voice, "Eloi, Eloi, lama sabachthani?" which means, "My God, my God, why have you forsaken me?"
>
> **Mark 15:34**

Other than the Aramaic, I understood that prayer. It was out front of all other considerations. "Why have you forsaken me?" Why? I had to know. "Are you there?" If God turned his back on his Son, then who am I? The most troubling question of all was still to come. Those I just mentioned were still warm on my lips when I asked, "Is there really a loving God out there?" This question, as desperate as it is, triggered a whole series of questions like it, questions I never thought I would dare to ask. I had no answer, nor was I even sure I wanted one. They were a bit dangerous, but maybe that is the point. Perhaps this is the exact place I needed to be, the posture I needed to be in to learn something or to be transformed. That is, I think, the whole purpose of our suffering—transformation. Desperation becomes a Mount of Transfiguration itself. After all, it is to the desperate that God responds, that place where all you have or all that is left to do is trust in the supreme love and power of our heavenly Father, the trust that Scripture declares is blind, unencumbered by care, debate, or second thought. Faith has eyes that reach beyond the natural. After all, it was a bloody persecution, a severity we can hardly imagine, that gave the early church its start. Desperation, in the care of God, has benefits we might never consider, bright and healthy ones.

Desperation clears the mind of debris, strips it down to essentials. Desperation is a powerful charm between God and man.

David Teems, *And Thereby Hangs a Tale* **(Harvest House)**

I wish I could tell you that my faith never wavered during this period of my life and that I knew everything would be all right. But I can't. There are not enough adjectives to describe the pain, the loneliness, the confusion, and the abandonment I felt. I knew in my heart that I had to keep going, I just didn't know how. I kept praying. Even when I felt like an idiot for my pains, I kept at it. It was all I knew to do, all I had left. Slowly, my prayers, like me, changed. They went from "Fix this!" to "Show me what to do!" Panic slowly turned to peace, or something close to peace. It was a start. My questions changed from "Why?" or "How?" to "What?" as in, "What do you want me to do? I long to do your will." Instead of focusing on what I didn't have, I started to look at what I had been given. Again, it was a start.

I found a church and began to immerse myself in worship every chance I could. I started attending Divorce Care classes to learn how to heal. I went to Al-Anon group meetings to work on myself. (Yes, alcohol is part of this sad country song.) I developed an appetite for books. I began going to personal counseling. I started writing music again. I went on daily walks through nature. I walked by streams and lakes, on trails that meandered through the woods of Tennessee. In short, I started to heal. I talked to God on these walks. Never once did I hear his audible voice, but it no longer mattered. On many of these walks, I asked him to show me he was there, that I was not alone. One day a soft breeze touched my face in just the right way. I knew it was him. Some might say I imagined it. Let them. I had a new hope. I was taking the first steps of a new beginning.

Now faith is confidence in what we hope for and assurance about what we do not see.

Hebrews 11:1, NIV

Am I the same person today that I was at the beginning of 2013? In some ways, perhaps. But in a more significant way, I am not. Has my faith in God changed? Yes, it has. Many of the truths I lived by, those that had shaped me for so long, were undone, overthrown. In some cases, they were completely destroyed that year. Am I better for it? My response is a resounding *yes*!

Does that mean at the end of this tale I might somehow glorify or make an idol of the pain I went through? No, it does not. Clarity and sobriety are wonderful things, hard-won and hard-bought as they are. Both come at a price. So what? Once purchased, they give God access, immediate and timely. He has his reasons.

[God] comforts us in all our troubles so that we can comfort others. When they are troubled, we will be able to give them the same comfort God has given us.

2 Corinthians 1:4 (NLT)

I doubt there are enough pages to list all the miracles that took place those first couple of years after my return to Nashville. And that is all I know to call them—miracles. What else could they be? My ears were poised to listen, my heart to take in and to process every lovely syllable from his mouth. Too many times I called out to God, wanting to hear a booming James Earl Jones voice in all caps cry out, "I AM HERE!" I might have given up the ghost right then and there had that happened. Granted, there may be times he has to be loud, but you will know that too. It was in my grief, in the depths of my loneliness, at the very ragged end of myself and in the long death of my old life that I heard him with a clarity I could never have imagined, and with the sparkle, sheen, and polish you would have to recognize as his own.

CRICKETS

Randy Finchum and Kent Maxson

My bills are bigger than the checks I'm getting,
The rumor is the shop will be shutting down.
Some days I feel like giving up and quitting.
I'm listening for your voice as I cry out,
"Where are you now?"

> **CHORUS**
> 'Cause all I hear are crickets
> And the evening breeze blowing through the trees.
> I send you prayers from on my knees,
> Begging you, God, please talk to me.
> If you've answered, Lord, I must have missed it.
> Are you near? 'Cause all I hear are crickets.

I came out here to do a little thinking,
Lay in the grass and stare up at the sky.
If you exist, why do you keep me waiting?
Do you care if your children live or die?
Why do I even try?

> **CHORUS**
> 'Cause all I hear are crickets
> And the evening breeze blowing through the trees.
> I send you prayers from on my knees,
> Begging you, God, please talk to me.

If you've answered, Lord, I must have missed it.
Are you near? 'Cause all I hear are crickets.

BRIDGE
I thought I'd hear you in the thunder—
A big voice up in the sky.
I never dreamed you'd speak so softly,
Like a whisper in the night.

CHORUS
And now I hear you in those crickets
And the evening breeze blowing through the trees.
I send you prayers from on my knees,
But I hear you when you talk to me.
You've always answered, Lord, I just missed it.
I know you're near, 'cause now I hear you in the crickets.
Oh, Lord, I hear you in the crickets.

Chapter 2

The Science of Optics (or Lipstick on a Pig)

The sun will rise and the wind will blow,
The rain will fall and the flowers grow.
Why? No one knows.

Kent Maxson and JK Nick Nichols, "The Rain Falls"

When I was a boy, I used to beg my dad to let me help mow the lawn. I was not yet big enough to push the mower myself, so he would place my hands on the bar while he pushed the mower. I thought I was big stuff. When I was old enough, he showed me how to prime the pump, pull the cord, attach the bag, and cut the grass like he did. I was thrilled at last to mow the lawn by myself. Sadly, the thrill didn't last as long as I had expected.

When I became a teenager, the last thing I wanted to do was get up on a Saturday morning and mow the lawn. But if I wasn't at it by 9 a.m., my dad would come into my room and yank the covers off my bed with a loud, "Time to cut the grass!" He seemed to get a charge out of that. I wasn't amused. Cutting the grass, a thing I had marveled at as a small boy, had lost its allure by the time I was old enough to manage it myself.

When I graduated from college and moved to Nashville in 1983, I found surprisingly few job openings for budding country music stars. I had to find some other way to pay the bills. Irony notwithstanding, I ended up cutting grass to put food on the table and to pay the bills. In a short time, I discovered that mowing a lawn or two for pay wasn't all that bad. And I liked working outside, working on my tan, getting a little exercise. It was much better than stocking shelves in a grocery store. In the span of a few years, therefore, my attitude toward mowing a lawn changed, taking me from wild and joyful expectation in my childhood to drudgery in my teens, then at last to acceptance as a young adult.

The point is my perspective changed. My dad, long before I had any perspective at all on anything, had not just equipped me to mow a lawn, which he did very effectively, but he also corrected my vision, so to speak, that I might understand how practical and how beneficial learning a skill can be. There were many lessons in those few exchanges, too many to enumerate here, but in his way, he helped to shape my perspective, to clear the film of youth from my eyes.

A friend of mine once told me a story about a car crash at a busy intersection in the city where he lived. When the police arrived, they asked the first driver to give them the details of what had happened. Next, they interviewed the second driver for his version of the events. Finally, they found a pedestrian who was standing at the corner of the intersection and saw the whole thing. Each version was different. Although each person shared what they honestly thought had happened, each had a different frame of reference. Their views were accurate from their perspectives.

One of the questions for which an answer seems improbable, and therefore begs perspective, may be "Why do bad things happen to good people?"

Before attempting the impossible, the question itself can be turned on its heels, so one might ask "Why do good things happen to bad people, or bad things to bad people?" And so on. Of course, there are many opinions to sort through, and in the greater analysis what is most necessary in the face of that question is, once again, perspective. To sermonize on judging who is good and who is bad, or why this or that happens to someone, is tricky business. There are snares in it, the awareness of which *is* perspective, the adjustment and correction of sight. Anyway, while perspective doesn't make such questions go away, it does often put them in their place.

> As it is written: "There is no one righteous, not even one; there is no one who understands; there is no one who seeks God. All have turned away, they have together become worthless; there is no one who does good, not even one."
>
> **Romans 3:10–12, NIV**

Something twists in me, if just a little, when I read that passage. It reminds me how much I need to tend to my own house, to the man in the mirror—that is, me. Like you, I am complicated flesh, and it is so easy at times for those complications to get the better of me, to get in my way. Those are the times I need perspective most, when I need something or someone greater than myself, greater than my complications, to bring me back. That very awareness, again, is perspective. It is like having a guard over your thought life, a presence that can speak to you in the unclear moment, even as Scripture says, "Whether you turn to the right or to the left, your ears will hear a voice behind you, saying, 'This is the way; walk in it'" (Isaiah 30:21, NIV). That both comforts and liberates me. Like desperation, the arousal and exercise of perspective clears the heart and mind of clutter.

Perspective is sight adjusted and corrected, the degree of clarity by which you see, including all angles and distances, how you perceive and understand something, the lens through which we process what we see. The *Oxford English Dictionary*, in an older definition of the word, refers to perspective as "the science of optics, as used in assisting sight." I love that definition. By science, we mean looking under the hood, so to speak, going deep inside a thing, taking note of how it works—the mechanics, its internal architectures, its minute particulars, what it runs on, what makes it tick.

LIKE THE ROLL OF A QUIET SEA

Optics, in today's vernacular, is how something looks. Politicians are masters at optics, or they strive to be, especially when they attempt to bend the truth mightily or tell that little white lie. To abuse a popular idiom, optics are at times just lipstick on a pig. With bright lights, shiny objects, and beautiful convincing language, you can sell anyone almost anything. Correct vision is the only defense against this, whether it comes from preacher or politician, teacher or the nightly news. Because we are such a visual culture, more coin is spent on how something looks than on any other aspect. Take care. Keep your lens clean and your perspective polished.

The gospels offer a good example of perspective, being four interpretations, or angles, of the same event: the life, ministry, death, and resurrection of Christ. The best definition this venerable old dictionary (*OED*) cites for the word *perspective* is "the true understanding of the relative importance of things; a realistic sense of proportion." I think of my dad, with a slight grin on his face, the lawnmower purring beside him.

For the believer, and according to the words of Jesus himself, John 14:6 makes it very clear in the simplest terms that Jesus alone *is* our perspective, our vision—most particularly when we have none. But even better than that, your perspective, your vision of life, becomes refined by him and is tuned to a perfect pitch. To put it in the first person, as Jesus does, he says, "I am the way," which is to say *I am the path laid out before you, the North Star to all your wandering.* "I am the truth," he adds, *the measure against which your opinions, the heart of every thought, every imagination should be weighed.* "I am the life," to complete the passage. *I am the very soul and DNA of all good, of all those stray thoughts and opinions that need guidance and trajectory.*

We live in a fallen world. There is no tiptoeing around that; once Adam took a bite of the apple, everything changed. But go easy on the poor guy. Before the fall, he didn't have to work so hard for perspective. It was in the air that he breathed, in the water he drank. It sparkled in the light around him. He walked with God in the cool, the very cool of the day. How cool is that? Yet when faced with a grave decision, he faltered. So what? I don't dare hurl a stone or anything else at the poor creature, not from my little glass house. We are all Adam. Like him, we no longer live in a physical paradise. We have to work out our salvation. But that is the beauty of being who we are. The only real work is to become like Christ, who is not only the path back to Eden, but how we rediscover and regain our paradise in him.

> We don't yet see things clearly. We're squinting in a fog, peering through a mist. But it won't be long before the weather clears and the sun shines bright! We'll see it all then, see it all as clearly as God sees us, knowing him directly just as he knows us!
>
> **1 Corinthians 13:12, MSG**

There are billions of people on this planet, even as there are limitless false gods, all of which represent more perspectives, a mash of opinions. There are angels. There are demons. There are so many voices convincing you and me what is right and what is wrong, who or what is good, and who or what is bad. Clamor. Noise. Social media has essentially given everyone a voice, which is fine in some respects, perhaps, but very noisy in another. It makes one dizzy. What do you do with all the noise? How do you hold on to perspective once you have it? Instead of offering another mouthful of opinion, I will let Scripture address these questions.

> I am the LORD your God, who teaches you what is best for you, who directs you in the way you should go. If only you had paid attention to my commands, your peace would have been like a river, your well-being like the waves of the sea.
>
> **Isaiah 48:17–18, NIV**

How great is that? The LORD, in all caps, assures us that he is our instruction, our path forward, the end to anxious searching. The result is peace like a river, our righteousness as unstoppable and mysterious as the roll of a quiet sea. There is a price to pay, certainly, if we refuse to pay attention. He has his ways. And yes, those ways are mysterious (though sometimes less mysterious than others). Still, even in the midst of correction, he is God, he is our Father, our sanctuary, our quiet mind, our comfort and deep rest.

> My suffering was good for me, for it taught me to pay attention to your decrees.
>
> **Psalm 119:71, NLT**

> Sometimes it takes a painful experience to make us change our ways.
>
> **Proverbs 20:30, GNT**

But God teaches people through suffering and uses distress to open their eyes.

Job 36:15, GNT

Now I am glad I sent it, not because it hurt you, but because the pain caused you to repent and change your ways.

2 Corinthians 7:9, NLT

A SPIRITUAL RUBIK'S CUBE

Through experience, I have come to realize one truth about being hurt: Pain alters you. If you touch a hot stove, you learn very quickly to stop placing your hand on it. You no longer have to labor in thought, seek counsel, pray about it, pace the floor, or anything else because your next response to the thing has become visceral, autonomic. When a friendship ends, perhaps because you were untrustworthy or couldn't keep a secret, you experience pain. If that pain is intense enough, it will cause you to examine your behavior and realize your fault—that you sabotaged something precious, something you may not get back. Reconciliation, if possible, will not be easy. And even if it's attempted, the effort may bear no fruit. Your friend may cast you off. Even so, that doesn't mean you can't learn from the episode. If pain alters, grief cleanses. Another way of saying it: sorrow purifies. Depending on the severity of the pain, you will either choose to continue repeating the offense in other forms, or, with an adjustment of sight, allow change to do its deep work. If we are broken enough, surrendered enough, we may just find ourselves being shaped into the image of Christ.

When life is going well, it is easy to take blessings for granted. What is worse is when those blessings become synonymous with or perceived as entitlement, thinking ourselves so deserving that we have some right to all the good things—food, clothing, clean water, soft beds, money in the bank, nice house, nice car, freedom from toil, and so on. To walk upon so high a ledge is to not notice that to fall is to fall hard, and most often according to the height we placed ourselves at in the first place. We may tell ourselves God has deserted us. Woe is me.

> *Like the rain falls on everyone,*
> *The sun shines on everyone.*

In our confusion, we may even cry out angrily at God, perhaps considering it in some way his fault. Ah, but then the penny drops, so to speak, in that delicious and unsettling moment of clarity when we realize our assessment of the situation may be a wrong one—that is, if we allow it, if we are conscious enough, fortunate enough, awake enough, if we allow salvation to do its hard work of excellence in us. The noise dissipates. We are left alone with ourselves. If, in that instant, our perspective has made all the right adjustments, if it has been tuned to Christ, we bow our heads, realizing our part in all this, the transgression plain before us. If you are quiet enough, still enough, you may just hear the following lyric, drawn from the depths of Scripture, uttered, as it was, in response to an entire people in want of perspective:

> Shout for joy, you heavens; rejoice, you earth; burst into song, you mountains! For the LORD comforts his people and will have compassion on his afflicted ones. But Zion said, "The LORD has forsaken me, the Lord has forgotten me." "Can a mother forget the baby at her breast and have no compassion on the child she

has borne? Though she may forget, I will not forget you! See, I have engraved you on the palms of my hands; your walls are ever before me..."When I came, why was there no one? When I called, why was there no one to answer? Was my arm too short to deliver you? Do I lack the strength to rescue you. . ." For a brief moment I abandoned you, but with deep compassion I will bring you back. In a surge of anger I hid my face from you for a moment, but with everlasting kindness I will have compassion on you," says the LORD your Redeemer.

Isaiah 49:13–16; 50:2; 54:7–8, NIV

Pay close attention to those words, you who wish to sharpen your vision! How many of us have felt what Israel felt, feeling forsaken and forgotten by God. His response comes in the form of a question: Can a mother forget the baby at her breast? It is a love you cannot make happen or not happen, any more than you can understand it. It just is. According to the King James Bible, he is the I AM. That's his name. I AM THAT I AM. In all caps. He is the one who *is*. In another translation of that same passage in Exodus 3, sixteenth-century English Bible translator William Tyndale (1494–1536) interprets the passage this way: "I will be what I will be. Tell them I will be has sent you." In the economy of God, he is both the I AM THAT I AM and the *I will be what I will be*. Can we figure such a thing out? No. And I am not sure we are supposed to. It's a spiritual Rubik's cube. Figuring it out is wide of the point anyway. We simply trust what he says, that though mom may forget, *he* will not. His very next word is all about perspective. *See.* As in, "See, I have engraved you on the palms of my hands." The hands of Jesus are marked with signs of his commitment to us, are they not? Is not your name and mine written there, written in the scars? How is that for perspective?

There are reasons he says what he says when he says it, and not just for a people far removed from you and I, a remote gaggle of sheepherders and the like on the other side of the world in the dusty foothills of Bronze Age Judea. No. His words have a much better, much longer reach than that, and through time itself. It is an old love that moves them, one we may enjoy but never truly comprehend. But only an enlightened or inspired perspective can assure you of such a thing. And as with any great love, mystery keeps the charm alive. Each syllable has unimaginable reach, right into your little life, into our little time, into my little thought life. Why? He tells us why.

> I have told you these things, so that in me you may have peace. In
> this world you will have trouble. But take heart! I have overcome
> the world.
>
> **John 16:33, NIV**

Well, that's a big fat comfort. Trouble? Who wants that? This question begs a little perspective. To say "in this world you will have trouble" isn't to say that it is something he puts on us, that you should stand aloof from me because at any moment lightning may strike me down and you don't want to be anywhere near me. That's as silly as it sounds. But because we live in a fallen world, we are going to get hit with the shrapnel of it, of those who live and believe very differently than you do, or with just the slings and arrows of life itself. We are going to lose people we love. We are going to ache with loss. Like Christ, we are going to bruise, and perhaps bleed on occasion, suffer injustice, and so on. If it rains, it is going to rain on the just and the unjust, the good and the bad. Remembering also that the name *Israel* itself means *to struggle with God and to overcome.* Struggle, therefore, is written into the name.

We are going to experience the unspeakable. While it is not his doing, the mending is all his. It is his business, so to speak. *We* are his business. Our perspective can and will be tampered with, tested, and tried, simply because it is subject to contamination and decay. At the same time, he says don't fret over it, that it is not only common and natural, it is necessary. And know this: If your perspective, your vision of life and beyond, is subject to contamination and decay, it is also subject to a kind of greatness, that greatness being God's, of course. Our thoughts, our speech, our charity, our warmth, our empathies, our possession of Christ—with our cooperation—can come under his management and instruction and begin to sparkle in ways that were once unimaginable. To take heart is to know the print of Christ on our lives, to know the peace that comes with surrender, surrender to the hard and yet outrageously sweet truth that he has conquered, that he has overcome the world, that the walls of your home are ever before him, that my troubles and yours are momentary, that any corruption in my faith or in my sight has no power over his love for me. Or for you.

Like the rain falls on everyone / the sun shines on everyone.

THE RAIN FALLS

Kent Maxson, Nick Nichols

He's got a blanket for walls with a cardboard roof,
Sleeps in the alley back of Third Street and Spruce.
Every morning on the corner he stands with his sign,
Begging for a dollar, but he rarely gets a dime.
But the rain falls on everyone,
Yeah, the rain falls on everyone.

Six-figure income in his three-piece suit,
Picks off the lint and scans the financial news.
Winston drives him to the corporate jet,
Holds his umbrella so he don't get wet.
But the rain falls on everyone,
Yeah, the rain falls on everyone.

> The sun will rise and the wind will blow,
> The rain will fall and the flowers grow.
> Why, no one knows.

The day is fading as the streetlights start to hum.
A car drives by then slowly backs up.
The glass goes down, there's a twenty-dollar bill.
It's been some time since he last had a meal.
And the sun shines on everyone,
Yeah, the sun shines on everyone.

It took one call to turn around that plane.
The deal went south, and guess who's to blame.
He caught a cab, that same phone rang:
"Hey, Dad, you coming to my basketball game?"
And the sun shines on everyone,
Yeah, the sun shines on everyone.

Like the rain falls on everyone,
The sun shines on everyone.
Like the rain falls on everyone,
The sun shines on everyone.

Chapter 3
Forget the Eggs

I will hold your hand, together we will stand.

Even if you find you need to hide away,

I will be by your side.

I will be by your side.

Kent Maxson and Adam James Deiboldt, "By Your Side"

When my kids were little, we lived in a house with a stairway that led to the second floor where their bedrooms were. About five feet up the stairway was a small landing area. At this point, the stairs made a sharp turn, and they continued up to the second floor. Not long after we moved into this house, the kids and I created a game. They would run up to this landing area and yell for me to come and catch them as they jumped into the air like superheroes and into my arms. I enjoyed their squeals as they flung their tiny bodies through the air. They always trusted me to catch them as they took turns jumping into my arms, and they would have been content to play this game nonstop for hours. I marveled at the faith each of them had in me—an unquestionable faith, innocent and without reserve, knowing I would be there to catch them.

One day I returned home with my arms full of groceries. As I brought them into the house, I heard my youngest daughter yell, "Daddy, catch me!" I looked over my shoulder just in time to see her fling her tiny 3-year-old body into the air with nothing to break her fall to the tile floor. I had only a split second to decide what to do. Without thinking, I dropped the bag of groceries, eggs and all, and managed to grab her about six inches from the floor. My heart racing wildly, I collapsed on the floor. Of course, she squealed with delight. After I regained my composure, I made sure she knew to never jump unless I told her I was ready to catch her. I lay there on the floor in shock at what had just happened. Forget the eggs.

She had no doubt that I would catch her. She was not yet the teenager, and I was not yet the Freddy Krueger of dads. At three, however, her trust in me was unshakeable, not yet tested. She knew her father would always be there for her. But what would she have thought had I not managed to catch her? What if I had hesitated? What if I had let her hit the ground? Would things have changed between us? Would she have ever trusted me again? Would trust itself be forever altered, held suspect?

Belief comes easy to a child. Innocence lives by a faith it little thinks of. Like God, it just *is*. That is why children reflect such a grand image of redemption; they doubt not the arms that will be there to catch them. "Suffer the little children to come unto me," Jesus said, "and forbid them not: for of such is the kingdom of God" (Mark 10:14, KJV).

It is much easier for a child to have the faith to leap off a stairway into their father's arms than it is for a parent to have faith in a loving God when sitting in a hospital watching their child struggle for life. While that may seem an unfair or extreme comparison, the parallel is an accurate one. When someone is visible, when they are by your side or at least close enough and strong enough to catch you when you fall, game or not, and have proven it over and over again, it is reasonable to think it will always be that way, that those arms will always perform their fatherly duty. But when your child or your spouse is fighting for their life and you feel helpless, it presents a challenge of faith and trust that is unbearable and tells us more about ourselves than we are perhaps prepared to know. How do you believe there is an invisible God within reach when your pain is so great that you see no evidence that he cares, or that he's even there at all?

And behold, I am with you always, to the end of the age.
Matthew 28:20

A teacher once told me there is no such thing as an absolute. Upon first consideration, I suppose she had a point, as sour as that point may have been. She may as well have said God is a myth, but she didn't go that far. She might have said when you fall you are on your own. What I got out of it was that while humanity does its best, even at its best it is fallible. What an interesting word: *fallible*. And with what precision it fits in this context. A quick peek at the *Oxford English Dictionary* once again: *fallible* is a variant of *fallable*, which means "capable of falling (in various senses); liable to fall." Of course, falling is not the same as jumping. My daughter did not fall; she jumped into my arms. Innocence does that. Innocence can jump. It cannot yet differentiate the serious from the play, so all is play. As adults, we are not so fortunate, not nearly as sure. Still, what an image of faith it demonstrates! How I envy her, even this far downstream. But the hard truth is there are few at this end of life who are going to drop the eggs for me or for you. Some will try, certainly, and may even succeed. Some will make the attempt to catch you but fail under the sheer weight. At least they tried, right?

When it comes to falling, I think it safe to say it is not a matter of *if* we fall, but *when*. And when I fall, will there be any "everlasting arms" to catch me? Looking back at my teacher, you might imagine her being let down at some point in her life, perhaps tragically, and what faith she might have had in humanity, in God, or in the world around her shattering when she hit the ground. Maybe she fell in love with no safety net beneath her. Broken trusts. Broken hearts. Broken vows. The images are countless. There are a lot of us like my old teacher, who perhaps leaned too hard and with exaggerated trust in those everlasting arms. By the way, if you are not familiar with that phrase, imagine a country church, an old piano, a song leader, no air conditioning, creaky old oak pews, stained glass, blue-haired old ladies, paper fans, and lots and lots of voices.

> *What have I to dread, what have I to fear,*
> *Leaning on the everlasting arms;*
> *I have blessed peace with my Lord so near,*
> *Leaning on the everlasting arms.*
> *Leaning, leaning,*
> *Safe and secure from all alarms;*
> *Leaning, leaning,*
> *Leaning on the everlasting arms.*

LOVE IS NOT A PLAYTHING

These are hypothetical constructs, provable only by time and circumstance, but even the most trusted of friends can, and will, fail us. It is one of those lessons we all learn as we transcend the toys of our youth and bloom into adulthood. We learn by increment, step by step, experience by painful experience, what trust is truly all about. We may even have some understanding of faith long before we come to Christ. That is perhaps why it is difficult for so many, faith being abused as it often is by the time we are grownups.

Sustainable truth in a broken world is like that apple of gold in settings of silver, to borrow from a proverb. We only experience everlasting, unbreakable truths and promises when God breaches the gap between him and us. Since most of what we experience in this world is broken, it is hard for us to believe in the exception. Yet all our hopes start with the knowledge and belief that God keeps his promises.

For me to pretend to know how God works, how he thinks, or why he does what he does is laughable. I can piece together conclusions based on his Word and the promises he has made to me, not to mention personal experience. But when all the dust settles, I believe in an all-supreme God, in a loving God, whose ways are far beyond what I can know or understand.

> Fear not, for I am with you; be not dismayed, for I am your God;
> I will strengthen you I will uphold you with my righteous right hand.
>
> **Isaiah 41:10**

Does his promise of always being there mean that nothing bad will happen? Hardly. Does it mean we will not experience pain as we journey through life? Again, not likely. To follow Christ, to be shaped in his image and tuned to the measures of his word, is to become like him. The prophet said Jesus was a man of sorrows, acquainted with grief. But don't take my word for it.

> He was despised and rejected by mankind, a man of suffering, and familiar with pain. Like one from whom men hide their faces he was despised, and we held him in low esteem. Surely he

took up our pain and bore our suffering, yet we considered him punished by God, stricken by him, and afflicted. But he was pierced for our transgressions, he was crushed for our iniquities; the punishment that brought us peace was on him, and by his wounds we are healed. We all, like sheep, have gone astray, each of us has turned to our own way; and the LORD has laid on him the iniquity of us all. He was oppressed and afflicted, yet he did not open his mouth; he was led like a lamb to the slaughter, and as a sheep before its shearers is silent, so he did not open his mouth.

Isaiah 53:3–7, NIV

Paul, who had an advanced knowledge of his Lord, one purchased by his own suffering, events that shaped his knowledge of him and gave him words, said, "I want to know Christ—yes, to know and the power of his resurrection and participation, in his sufferings, becoming like him in his death, and so, somehow, attaining to the resurrection from the dead" (Philippians 3:10–11, NIV). To become like him is to become "like him in his death." All the lovely hymns, the soft music playing in the background, though it is not meant to deceive, it is perhaps at some level misleading. I remember how broken I felt when I gave my life to the Lord, how surrendered, or at least as surrendered as I understood it at the time. There is a moment you convince yourself that God is going to take care of all your needs. And don't get me wrong, for the significant needs, the ones only he can supply, he does just that. But our life is a product of good decisions and not-so-good decisions. That is to say, the passage from one life to the next is not all bliss, music, and candlelight. The change, as many of you know, doesn't come overnight. But the promise, nonetheless, is true and dependable. It may be one of the few certainties you can count on in the life of faith.

There may be times when it seems that he doesn't drop the eggs and lets us fall. But that is by appearance only. As Paul demonstrated—and thousands, if not millions, like him since—the price is costly. It will literally cost you everything. None of this is meant to frighten or alarm, only to suggest that following Christ is a serious consideration to be taken seriously. The poet John Keats once said, "Love is not a plaything." He meant it. Paul meant it, as did Peter and countless others who paid dearly for their commitment to Christ—all of whom considered this present life of little value compared to the life to come. They would say, and with confidence, that God can and will be there, as close as our next breath, arms open, loving and supporting us as we navigate this grand adventure of life. There is a difference between rescue and support, between saving and presence, and they are all his. His promises are without repentance.

> And Jesus came and spoke to them, saying, "All authority has been given to Me in heaven and on earth. Go therefore and make disciples of all the nations, baptizing them in the name of the Father and of the Son and of the Holy Spirit, teaching them to observe all things that I have commanded you; and lo, I am with you always, even to the end of the age."
> **Matthew 28:18–20, NKJV**

I started my college career as a mechanical engineering major at Texas Tech. I did not choose this major because I loved it. During my senior year in high school, assessment tests indicated that this field of study was where my strongest natural abilities were. I also thought that being an engineering student would be more acceptable and respected by family and friends than being a music major. My parents did not force me into this decision, but it was not difficult to guess what their preference was. I did fine my first couple of years, but the further I got into my studies, the more I knew it was not for me. Being the pragmatic and sensible twenty-year-old that I was, I stopped attending class. Instead of finishing out the semester and changing my major, I just stopped. I replaced my class time with sitting in my dorm room every day, practicing the guitar and writing songs.

About a week after I came home for Christmas break, my report card arrived. I will never forget my mother's facial expression or the words she said when she opened my report card. In shock and disbelief, she said, "Why Kent, you've been kicked out of college." On a 4.0 scale, I had received a 0.50 GPA for the semester. I like to tell people that you don't just get a 0.50 GPA; you earn it. Nor did Texas Tech think too highly of my efforts. They informed me, bluntly, that I had been suspended from college for the next semester, and if I chose to return to college sometime later in the future, I would be on academic suspension.

I hurried off to my room, shut the door, and sat on my bed, awaiting my imminent death, which I was sure would happen when my dad got home from work. While I waited, one by one, my three sisters came into the room and tried to comfort me. Each of them said some form of, "It will be OK, Bubba." My mom came and silently brought me my last meal, a tuna fish sandwich. The family dog came in and licked me on the face. Each of them, including the dog, gave me their support and said what felt like their final goodbyes to me.

Poor Bubba.

I heard the garage door rise and lower, and the unmistakable sound of my father's footsteps as he walked into the kitchen. I waited for the executioner to come into my room. The question wasn't if I would die but rather how quickly and mercifully he would make my final moments on this earth. After what seemed like an eternity, I heard the doorknob slowly turn.

Poor Bubba.

He walked over and stood in front of me, and said calmly, "It looks like you had a rough semester." I did not respond. My head hung low, not wanting to look up. Then he said something I never expected him to say. "You know I didn't exactly tear up school in the beginning either. Now we will see what you are made of." He then turned around and quietly left my room. As long as I live, I will never forget that moment. My father didn't rescue me from the self-inflicted pain I had caused. He simply told me that he was with me. He wasn't going to rescue me from the results of the decisions I had made, but I knew he loved me. As if to say, "I'm not going to fix this; that's up to you. But I am here with you." Like the song says:

> Sometimes, we find, we just don't know
> We get caught in playing a role
> If you feel lonely there in the crowd,
> All you have to do is reach out
>
> I will hold your hand, together we will stand
> Even if you find you need to hide away
> I will be by your side,
> I will be by your side

Kent Maxson and Adam James Deiboldt, "By Your Side"

Fear not, for I am with you; be not dismayed, for I am your God; I will strengthen you, I will help you, I will uphold you with my righteous right hand.

Isaiah 41:10

Unlike my dad, God can and has rescued me from the eternal consequences of my sin. Of that I am certain. But there is still payment due, one way or another, temporary discomforts I will have to deal with from the result of poor choices. Did God really abandon me when I spent my cash on meaningless pursuits? Can I blame him for my poor health after a lifetime of choosing the wrong food and drink? I have been given complete freedom to make whatever choices I want to make. As much as we cherish freedom, it can be a devil in its own right if we take it too far or handle it irresponsibly. Still, because my choices led to pain does not mean God has abandoned me. I know better. He is still there. His love for me is unwavering as I deal with the results of my choices.

As much as I love my daughters, there is no way I can shield them from the sorrows of life. Like their dad, many times the pain my daughters experience is from poor choices they have made. I have one daughter who made the decision to drive while she was intoxicated. Thankfully, the only thing damaged that night was our car. They placed her in jail overnight. I was told she would be let out the next day. I waited in the lobby of the jail, wondering what I should do and say to her. I could tell by the look on her face she was shocked to see me and was also worried about what I would say. To my own surprise, I did not raise my voice or say anything about what had happened, her safety being the most pressing thing on my heart. I just told her we were going to take a ride.

I took her to where the accident had occurred. I showed her where she had left the road and where she had crashed. Then I drove her to the salvage yard. We got out of the car, and I took her to a pile of metal—the one that had once been the family car. "We can replace this car," I said. "What we can't replace is you. I hope you've learned something from this. Now we will see what you are made of." We went home, and she lay in her bed quietly for the rest of the day.

No Way Out But Through

I choose to believe that this moment in her life was a starting point for making better choices. After that, she made some good choices and some she regretted, as we all do. But she had learned a valuable lesson. She also knew her mother and I were there for her—and always would be. Love does not fix the bad choices we make. It does, however, provide strength for us to move on, to play the grownup, even as it helps us to heal. Love brings us back and shows us what we are made of.

THE QUIET HEART

I have always struggled with anxiety, so for me to give advice to the anxious seems a touch hypocritical. Understanding a problem does not mean you can solve it, but I can tell you what experience has taught me. Anxiety is usually based on some exaggeration, on overthinking, on leaning on my own understanding, or having suffered a breach of faith and ignoring the everlasting arms. The monsters under the bed are most often of our own creation. Some have teeth and will validate our fear. Some, if not most, are toothless, having little power to do much more than rattle or gum me to death. Like most of us who deal with anxiety, I have moments of success and moments of failure. The successes for me always come when I have the wit and strength to turn my slightest fear over to God, who is my shield, my rock, my redeemer, my good medicine. But that takes trust, which eludes my grasp on occasion. Again, the anxious deal more with the appearance of threat than with threat itself. At rock bottom, it is a matter of faith or the absence of it.

If I obsess over some issue, some fabricated monster against which I feel powerless, the real mistake for me would be to try to take the responsibility away from God, to attempt to take his place or do his job, thinking I can deal sufficiently with the crisis. Truth is, I have no control over anything except the choices I make, the good ones as well as the boneheaded ones. It is amusing, in its way, but each little skirmish with faith does what my father said long ago it would do: It shows me what I am made of. If we are wise at all, we learn, we process, we change, and we move forward—somehow better for our pains. To find peace, I must choose wisely and to trust in the God I profess to believe in.

Worrying is a control issue. When I worry, I am unconsciously stating that I want to be in control, that I want to slip into shoes that I know are way too big for me. I worry because I think I can do a better job than God. I worry because I have more faith in my own omnipotence than I do in God's. So, what should I do in these moments, particularly when my own self-deception has done its strange work? I can cry out. I can pray to God and trust that he will answer in spite of my folly. Ultimately, I need to know, accept, and trust who really is in control. Why do I keep putting God to the test? Why must God keep proving to me that he is there with me? It really does come down to faith, about who to trust, about keeping a watch over our tongue (a nice way of saying it's best to keep one's mouth shut). The quiet heart is what we're after, and the pursuit of the quiet heart is only possible with God. Scripture says clearly that like a father who loves his child, he is ever with you, and he will quiet you with his love. You can trust that.

> The Lord your God is with you, the Mighty Warrior who saves.
> He will take great delight in you; in his love he will no longer
> rebuke you, but will rejoice over you with singing.
>
> **Zephaniah 3:17, NIV**

When I was a young father, my wife and I took our children to see Santa Claus at the local mall. The older girls, with no hesitation, jumped up into Santa's lap and gave him their long list of toys they wanted for Christmas. My youngest daughter was afraid to approach the man—the white-bearded, jolly, and preposterously overweight stranger dressed in holiday red. Ho-ho-ho, all of it. It didn't matter that he had candy for every child or that her sisters didn't seem bothered by him. She was determined not to sit in his lap. That is until I walked with her. That was all it took. She felt safe as long as I was within arms' reach.

I try to remember this picture whenever I am afraid: No matter what bills are owed, no matter what calamity is broadcast on the news, no matter what unknown outcome is waiting for me the next day, I know I am safe. No matter the circumstances, my heavenly Father is that immediate, that close. Or closer.

Faith is a gift, alive and overflowing with life. It is never static, but always in motion, like the currents of air or the roll of the sea. It is not a diploma. I do not earn it. I am certain I don't understand it. Like God, faith too simply *is*. At the same time, it is ever becoming, in that *I will be what I will be* sense mentioned earlier, ever fixed yet ever reaching into the distance, stillness and movement, possession and chase, having and pursuing. It sounds a lot like being in love, which is the best understanding of it. Therefore, cherish it. Put it to use. Let love put you to use. Exercise it. Surrender your life to its will and do your best to have some ascendancy or government over your own. Be vigilant over love, protect it with what power you have, and allow it to protect you in the moment you are weak or blind. Relish every moment you have it, conscious or unconscious, mindful of the one who gave it to you. Trust it to show you what you are made of.

BY YOUR SIDE

Adam James Deiboldt, Kent Maxson

Sometimes, we all feel so alone
And daytime is nighttime if it's anytime at all
Takes all you've got to reach through the dark
Feels like life should not be this hard

> **CHORUS**
>
> I will hold your hand, together we will stand
> Even if you find you need to hide away,
> I will be by your side,
> I will be by your side

Sometimes, we find we just don't know
We get caught in playing a role
If you feel lonely there in the crowd,
All you have to do is reach out

> **CHORUS**
>
> I will hold your hand, together we will stand
> Even if you find you need to hide away,
> I will be by your side,
> I will be by your side

Chapter 4
How Could We Call It Anything But Love?

When I say "I love you," it's never enough
The words in my heart come out all mixed up
I want a better way to say what we both know
I want a new way to say something old

Kent Maxson and Marc Roberts, "Something Old"

Perched on an old tobacco stand in my bedroom is a mantel clock made in the early eighteen hundreds. As old as it is, not only does it still work, and with a perfect pulse, it lets you know it. It is not a quiet creature. Whenever I wind it up, the sound of the ticks and the tocks, though precise and regular, fill the entire house. Not only that, but every half hour it chimes to let you know what time of day it is. Sleeping through the racket is a particular challenge. Because of the noise it generates, I rarely wind it up. On certain occasions, however, and I am not even sure I can tell you why, I crank the thing up and bring it back to life. A few turns of a key and I am transported back to a time when my grandmother was a young girl who stared at it very much the way I do now. This old clock is one of my most prized possessions. As you might guess, it has a story.

My grandmother's name was Violet. Having died when my father was a senior in high school, I never got to know her. Daddy was not one to share details about his feelings, especially when it came to his mom, so I always wondered what she was like, and why the mystery. My only knowledge of her came from a few things I could put together whenever my father spoke of her, if only in a slip of speech, from the few stories my grandpa told, and the pictures of her we kept in the closet in an old photo album. I used to stare at those pictures and marvel at how beautiful she was. One of the first songs I ever wrote was called "Violet," a haunting little tune that I believe captured the beauty and mystique of the grandmother I never knew.

When I was in junior high, after visiting my mother's parents in Kansas, we stopped in Amarillo, Texas, to visit my father's Aunt Gladys. I had never met her, and don't remember anyone mentioning her name before that trip. But when I found out she was my grandmother's younger sister, I couldn't wait to meet her. When we arrived at her house, I could hardly contain my excitement. My imagination wild with wonder and anticipation, I was smitten with her immediately. She was tiny, feisty, funny, and full of life. In her, I got small glimpses of my grandmother, if in little sparks of my great-aunt's personality. She told story after story and to a spellbound audience of one. Aunt Gladys and I became best friends.

When we returned home to Midland, I started writing her letters every few months. I didn't see her again until I went away to college at Texas Tech. My apartment in Lubbock was only a couple of hours drive from Amarillo. If I had a free day, I did my best to spend some time with her. Occasionally, I would spend the night and stay up late pelting her with question after question about her sister, Violet, as well as my great-grandfather, Andrew Campbell Reed. I have beautiful memories of our conversations as she gave life and movement to the faces I had seen in those old photo albums. Little by little, my grandma and great-grandpa became real to me.

On one of my first visits to her house, I noticed an old clock sitting on the fireplace mantel. I asked her about it. She said it had belonged to her father that when she was a little girl one of the big events for her and her nine siblings took place every night around this clock. Her father would call everyone to the kitchen table, and they would all watch as he took a feather and dripped kerosene into the gears of the clock to clean it. Every once in a while, he would let one of the older children take a turn as he supervised the process. I could almost see my grandma as a little girl, her eyes wide, fixed on the old man and the clock. It hit a lovely note in me how this old clock was and how at one time it was the center of a family ritual, generations deep, set around something as simple as time and a feather. Just like my family's television and the radio of my dad's youth, this clock was the communal hub of my ancestors.

Through the years, I maintained contact with Gladys. I always found her loving, supportive, insightful, and hilarious. When she passed away, she left me the entirety of her small estate, which included my great-grandfather's clock and the family Bible, against which no dollar value can be placed. She knew those things were safe with me.

Today, when we have guests in our house, almost everyone comments on the clock. It has that kind of presence. And, as I mentioned earlier, it is not a quiet creature. You just know it has a story, one with depth, character, and perhaps a touch of mysticism. Some have asked me what the old clock might be worth. When I had it appraised, I was told its value was around a couple of hundred dollars, an amount that had no real meaning to me whatsoever. Never did. To me, it was a door, a way back.

As a writer, some of you may think I am exaggerating or giving meaning to something that may not be there, something you might expect of a song or a poem. And you may be right at some level. I do my best to remain vigilant, on watch for the extraordinary when the extraordinary presents itself, especially when discovered among the ordinary. All I know is, by the grace, love, and foresight of a beautiful spirit, a sister to my grandmother, the clock was entrusted to me. The gaze of a child, the feather, the kerosene, the ritual, the great love, and old magic all made this timepiece priceless, gave it a place of honor, not only among my thoughts, but among all I possess. It offers a perfect introduction and illustration of what I wish to talk about presently: the difference between the actual value of something and its perceived value, including how it relates to time.

When I wrote the song "Something Old," I was thinking about how familiarity with someone can be a tricky thing. With all the electricity, the flirtation and giddiness, the sorcery of those first kisses, it is easy to get carried away, especially when passion takes precedence over reason. How could we call it anything but love? We want instant possession, every hour and minute. Love is as complex as it is beautiful, as full of caution as charm. We want possession, every hour and minute. So, what about love when it turns sour, or fails?

> *They walk hand in hand moving in time*
> *And there's nobody else in their world*
> *It's their first time in love, their last time alone*
> *Hanging on every word*
> *I remember a time when we were just like that*
> *Everything was new but I don't want to go back*

Even as I write this, I am reminded of all the countless writers and poets, all the lovers and craftsmen who have attempted the same thing—who, like me, have tried to put enchantment into words. Whether an actual poem, a sonnet, a letter, a hit song, a Hallmark romance, *You've Got Mail*, or the honeyed drip of a Nicholas Sparks novel, many have succeeded. But that is art, with its many strategic effects and pleasant fictions. What happens, however, when the newness of love wears off, when the heat begins to cool, and all the golden words are spent? What is left when the spark becomes a fizzle, when the adrenaline and dopamine are all spun out, leaving you not only sober but with a hangover of a kind? What happens when a poem, a letter, or a song can no longer keep love afloat? This is the moment when that tension between perceived value and actual value of the once glorious heart-stopping thing becomes painfully clear. Sadly, for many, it marks the end of the relationship, one that might have had a chance to bloom, but is now worn and ragged with use, and primarily because the foundation was not as solid as one may have thought. Based solely on feelings, pretty speech, or the cultivation of some fiction, however pleasant, it cannot last. Passion spends itself quickly. Longevity and true love depend on something else altogether, something immovable, much stronger and longer lasting than fascination. Or art.

SURRENDER IS THE POINT

True love is not an emotion. Emotion is fickle. It doesn't always tell the truth. Though poets and rhymers of all stripes have had much to say on the subject, and though the magic mentioned above is its biggest draw, at its very best, deepest, and truest, love is a surrender, one that strengthens and deepens, even as it sweetens with time.

In the summer of 1984, on the day of his wedding, a friend of mine said the following before God, a small group of friends, a minister, and his bride to be: "This day I put to death all other options." I am not sure an explanation is necessary, but for clarity's sake that simply means that his commitment to her and to their marriage was absolute. And though the absolute in our hands (or our vows) is often slippery and easy to abuse, that same friend will tell you, now forty years later, that the love he felt those many years ago, sealed with a few vows and a preacher's signature, was a mere bud. As new as it was in those first moments, as sacred, as newly sworn, unknown and untested, over time he established a home in his heart for her and has remained a vigilant watchman over that home since. Two sons and five grandchildren later, he will tell you that their relationship took on a bloom he could never have imagined, described, or thought himself capable of, that all the elements came together, as if by a script written somewhere and by a divine hand.

Surrender is the point. My life is no longer my own. It belongs to something greater than me, divinely appointed with all the validations of heaven, all the sacred chemistries, all the right attractions. Is it easy? In some ways *no*, it is not. Surrender of this kind, of this depth and magnitude is never easy, but the benefits are measureless. Does it take maintenance? Of course it does, daily and vigilant. But even that becomes sacred. I keep using the word surrender as if it is a one-time event, but like the peace of God or salvation itself, surrender is an ongoing enterprise. When you come to Christ, it is a marriage of a kind. We are the Bride of Christ, and though I will not elaborate even if I could, it suggests the kind of commitment Christ himself makes to you and me—one that transcends death itself. Love is the narrow path, and upon surrender you will desire no other path—the narrower, the better. The peace, like love itself, is immeasurable, secure, dependable, without flaw or condition, as trustworthy and deathless as it is unfathomable, and, as Scripture says, it is beyond our ability to define with mere words.

Whether a relationship with God or another human being, it is long love we are after. When I think of my grandfather's clock, I realize that telling time is only one thing it does now. When I look at it, I am transported back to the family kitchen table of my great-grandparents. I see the faces of each child as they watch Daddy perform the solemn ritual of cleaning the family clock. I hear the squirm and giggle of anticipation. And for a few moments, I am among them. I can hear them. It is an old love I feel, well populated, a love of profound depths, and it smiles sweetly upon me, a love of long and beautiful consequence with a reach generations beyond itself. By some mysterious transaction beyond our telling, my great-grandfather's clock has become something timeless and, in a sense, immortal. Isn't that what love should do for all of us? Only in love is it possible to know God in ways not allowed or hardly anticipated before.

> Anyone who does not love does not know God because God is love.
>
> **1 John 4:8**

BUT ONE DEATH AWAY

None of this excludes those who have no companion or those who may have chosen to remain single. Far from it. If I have somehow given the impression that this section of the book is only for those involved in romantic love, please read closer. Love is bigger than that. Paul had no wife. He was, however, intimately bound and surrendered to his Lord, Jesus Christ. And while we may speak of the Bride of Christ, Jesus had no earthly wife. Many of the followers of Jesus chose not to marry.

God is love. Scripture says so. It is his nature. He desires for us to share that nature, that we might love as he loves—that is, by the gift of self, a surrender that is as absolute as death, the all or nothing variety, allowing no other option, "for love is as strong as death" (Song of Solomon, 8:6). As mentioned earlier, love will cost something. There is no way around that.

But love makes the exchange an easy one, particularly once the light comes on, so to speak, and we become aware of what it means, of what God is all about. If I say it is but one death away, I do not mean physical death, but the death of our old life, of old ways of thinking, perceiving, and processing. God has done everything necessary to nourish and instruct each one of us in his love, that we may know and live by its redemptive power. Nor is it forced on anyone. Love isn't like that. Love that is forced must be called something else.

As mentioned earlier, on the cross, one of the last things Jesus cried out was, "My God, my God, why have you forsaken me?" (Mark 15:34, NIV). What if, just for the moment, those words were turned around and considered in another context? That is, what if they were directed at you, as if asked by the Lord: "Why have you forsaken me?" When aimed in *our* direction those words take on a whole new and unsettling intensity. I am not sure it needs more elaboration than that. To forsake him is to forsake self.

The notion of sacrifice is written into the highest form of the word *love* itself. Where English has one word for love and for any variation of it, in Greek there are eight different words used to describe eight different types of love. The highest of these is *agape*, which may be loosely defined as sacrificial, selfless, surrendered, without condition or repentance. This is the type of love God has shown us, that he wishes to cultivate in us—a love that is best given without expectation of anything in return.

A child crawls onto her father's or mother's lap and without formal invitation. Why? Because she is comfortable there. There is a bond of trust and nurture that makes her feel safe. She has been there many times without incident or correction, and she knows her father will drop the eggs on her behalf. We can develop the same relationship with God. Sadly, however, we have all witnessed the flip side of this transaction, that is, when someone gets too familiar, even with God. It happens. Ask Lucifer. He was the prince of heaven, the worship leader, the angel of light. There was none closer to the throne. But the heights of glory proved toxic for such a mind. He wanted more. His relationship with God wasn't enough, and we all know the result: Lucifer and his followers were cast out. He became haughty, arrogant. The result was disastrous.

How many modern preachers have you seen or heard of, who, with earthly success think they know better than God? They take it on themselves to build their own kingdom. And how many of them are then caught in some sexual or financial mishap, having abandoned the faith altogether? Worship becomes hollow spectacle. Recovery, while possible, can be devastating. This can only be attributed to the grace of God, but many of them are at last broken. In that brokenness many find themselves, regain themselves, and in that surrender are welcomed back at the Father's table.

Familiarity can breed contempt, as the saying goes, especially if that relationship is not nurtured correctly, with all the proper nutrients and medicines—the Word of God, the assembly of believers, good works, and so on. The above is a cautionary tale for all of us, whether you are a pastor, a husband, a wife, a friend, or a business associate. Distraction is your enemy. The blessed marriage, like a life dedicated to Christ, is an adventure, flesh and spirit, with all the pleasures of Eden (the word itself means *pleasure*). You cannot help but grow, individually and as a couple.

> You yourselves bear me witness, that I said, "I am not the Christ, but I have been sent before him." The one who has the bride is the bridegroom. The friend of the bridegroom, who stands and hears him, rejoices greatly at the bridegroom's voice. Therefore this joy of mine is now complete. He must increase, but I must decrease.

> **John 3:28–30**

In the passage above, John the Baptist declares that Jesus is the bridegroom. In the gospel of Mark, Jesus makes the same declaration, if obliquely.

> And Jesus said to them, "Can the wedding guests fast while the bridegroom is with them? As long as they have the bridegroom with them, they cannot fast. The days will come when the bridegroom is taken away from them, and then they will fast in that day."
>
> Mark 2:19–20

Complacency can lead to the slow death of faith, just as it can contribute to the slow death of a marriage. My dad once told me, "you don't stop courting your girl when you get married. It would be best if you courted your wife every day like it's your first date. Buy her flowers for no reason at all, send her cards, help with the kids, take her to dinner, wash the dishes. We may fumble a lot, but that is okay, too. We panic and scramble on Valentine's Day, combing the aisles of Kroger for a card and flowers. But take heart. As clueless as we are, gentlemen, knowledge of the effort itself is sometimes better than roses. Opening her car door or that random kiss is as good as a love song. She knows. She is smarter than you. Remember that." (Okay, I added a few personal tidbits, but my dad knew what he was talking about. He must have known something because he and my mother were married for sixty-eight years before he passed away.)

Adventure comes about by stepping out in faith. Just as a marriage needs to be continually nourished, so does our relationship with Jesus. Attending church every week is a good start, but sitting in a room full of people doesn't provide the same spark that living on the edge of faith does. Where do we find the spark? We find it by stepping out in faith into new experiences and cultivating the fruit from the older ones. We feed and strengthen faith with continuous exercise—small or large acts, it doesn't matter. Remembering the I AM THAT I AM and the *I will be what I will be* version of the Almighty means that he *is,* and he is also *becoming.* He is both constant and on the move at the same time. No, you can't figure it out either. Love behaves like that, like God. It may express itself through you by volunteering to cook meals for an elderly widower confined to an assisted living facility. It could be in serving as a sponsor for an orphan who has never known what a family is or, if possible, taking them into your home. It may be a gift of cash given anonymously to a struggling single parent, the more anonymous the better. I cannot tell you what act of kindness may keep the flame alive, but whatever it is, however visible or hidden, it will cause your love for God to grow. Both noun and verb, love is a state of being even as it is an action we take. Being and doing, it is immovable, fixed, as well as something that must be exercised. That is a poor definition, a close approximation, for some things defy explanation. Love is one of them.

> The steadfast love of the LORD never ceases; his mercies never come to an end; they are new every morning; great is your faithfulness.
>
> **Lamentations 3:22–23**

Do you not wish to share the life of God, the flow of light and wonder, in every transaction, including those with yourself? When overwhelmed by love, do you not wish to reciprocate it, to give some of it back, and in the giving receive even more? Don't let familiarity fool you into dullness or not doing your part. Again, you never have to earn your way into God's love; it is a gift that he freely gives you. But if you don't do your part to contribute to the relationship, you will be missing out on so much more. Keep the feather and the kerosene nearby and ready for use. The fascination is there already.

SOMETHING OLD

Kent Maxson, Marc Roberts

They walk hand in hand moving in time
And there's nobody else in their world
It's their first time in love, their last time alone
Hanging on every word
I remember a time when we were just like that
Everything was new but I don't want to go back

CHORUS

When I say "I love you," it's never enough
The words in my heart come out all mixed up
I want a better way to say what we both know
I want a new, way to say something old

The only thing that matters to me
Is spending my time with you
There's good times and bad that we both have had
That's just what lovers do
After all these years I still feel the same
And all these useless words they just don't explain

CHORUS

When I say "I love you" it's never enough
The words in my heart come out all mixed up
I want a better way to say what we both know
I want a new way to say something old

Chapter 5

The Sense It Makes

And the Word was God.

—John 1:1

I f anything has become clear in the making of this book, it is this: Christ is the ground upon which my story stands, sits, runs, or crawls about. He is the sense any of this makes or is likely to make. He provides the spine and good sense a book like this could only hope for. The following passage is one of the most repeated passages in the English language, and not just for its stature or command, its spiritual weight and meaning, but for expression itself, for the singularity of its sound, the lovely old voice by which it preaches, weeps, curses, woos, judges, prays, exalts, and shakes its fist—things it does beautifully. It is a proclamation of who Christ is. Like many passages of Scripture, it may not be the easiest one to understand at first, but some things are meant to be cultivated in us, realized in their own time.

> In the beginning was the Word, and the Word was with God, and the Word was God. He was with God in the beginning.

Through him all things were made; without him nothing was made that has been made. In him was life, and that life was the light of all mankind. The light shines in the darkness, and the darkness has not overcome it.

John 1:1–5, NIV

The prologue to the Gospel of John (above) is one of the best examples of context in Scripture. It not only settles who God is, it tells us the shapes our thoughts will take as we proceed, what governs or influences them, and how they will conform to his specifications. Christ, therefore, becomes the template, the blueprint of the successful life. Depending on how deep your investment and on other criteria known and unknown to us, in time we begin to think and respond like Christ. If you're like me, you're probably thinking, "I just wish it didn't take so long." Don't fret. His timing, like his plan, is perfect. In the grand cleanup, nothing is overlooked. All of it works together—our failures, our successes, all the hits and misses, all that is beautiful and ugly about ourselves, public and private. "All the days ordained for me," Scripture says, "were written in your book before one of them came to be" (Psalm 139:16, NIV).

Take heart, for he is as thorough as he is precise. When we feel farthest away from God, when it seems that things could not possibly get worse, it is during those times that your life is being written like a grand poem or a lovely piece of music, remembering that God is a creator, a poet, an artist, a songwriter—one who makes beautiful things, whose work is both fixed and ongoing. Here is a reminder of who he is and who you and I are to him, and how thoroughly attached:

Where can I go from your Spirit? Where can I flee from your presence? If I go up to the heavens, you are there; if I make my bed in the depths, you are there. If I rise on the wings of the dawn, if I settle on the far side of the sea, even there your hand will guide me, your right hand will hold me fast. If I say, "Surely the darkness will hide me and the light become night around me," even the darkness will not be dark to you; the night will shine like the day, for darkness is as light to you.

For you created my inmost being; you knit me together in my mother's womb. I praise you because I am fearfully and wonderfully made; your works are wonderful, I know that full well. My frame was not hidden from you when I was made in the secret place, when I was woven together in the depths of the earth, your eyes saw my unformed body; all the days ordained for me were written in your book before one of them came to be. How precious to me are your thoughts, O God! How vast is the sum of them! Were I to count them, they would outnumber the grains of sand—when I awake, I am still with you.

Psalms 139:7–18, NIV

When I awake, I awake to music.

I WAS THE FEATHER. IT WAS THE WIND.

Whether or not you have ever read a book, a pamphlet, a bumper sticker, or anything else, we are all aware of the narratives we live by, the stories that tell us who we are and show us the way through life. Many, if not most, of the narratives we live by are the ones we draft ourselves. This is natural, and it occurs whether you are conscious of it or not. Falling in love creates a narrative, as does developing a friendship, the work you do, the things you enjoy, all the many threads that hold life together, true, false, and so on. There is, perhaps, a narrative in your thoughts that pushes you forward, that inspires you. That narrative may be based on assumptions that are true, or assumptions about yourself that are totally fabricated. The point is, we do this all the time. We live by story, the one that brought us to a certain point in time and the one that is being created and revised in the moment and beyond. Like surrender, like faith, like love, it has an ongoing *I will be what I will be* kind of character about it. Our job, home life, private life, or relationships with others—all these things and more have their tale to tell, their contribution to make. Culture grows and evolves by way of story.

This storytelling is not only natural, it is both necessary and inevitable. We are in a state of composition all the time. It creates problems, however, when the narrative being spun around you directly opposes the truth of God or becomes contrary to that highly specialized narrative he has set in place for each of us before the world's creation. I realize this is a lot to take in, and I have gotten used to the thought that there are far more things for which I have no words than those things for which I do. Either way, I am at peace with what I don't know or cannot find speech for. That is not such a bad thing in this context.

A songwriter may have some awareness or perception (most often unconscious even for the songwriter) that eludes the theologian, things God may be able to entrust only to a psalm or a sonnet because of the musical way they bend, and with penetration far deeper than a sermon. Ask David the shepherd about that, or David the king. I will say more about it, but the Apostle Paul was, in my estimation, one of the finer poets who ever lived. He is certainly among the greatest of Bible writers. The poetry, the lyric of our lives I mentioned earlier, is the very way God has chosen to speak to us, the way he chooses to be explained (when there is explanation)—and that puts the songwriter on a level playing field with the theologian. The voice of God is primarily musical, rhapsodical, full of weight and splendor, things a poet has the ear for.

David was a man after God's own heart (1 Samuel 13:14). His heart was shaped after God's, fashioned with the kind of precision and delicacy that allowed David to speak directly to God and in the language God placed in him, that is, by way of a love song. Another meaning of 1 Samuel 13:14 suggests that David sought God vigilantly and with great intensity, that he was "after" God as one might chase "after" something or someone in pursuit. It was continuous in both the shepherd and the king. Good, bad, ugly, or otherwise, David held nothing back. His best music often came when he was distressed. The tragic line from Psalm 22, "My God, my God, why . . ." was a sentiment so powerful and said what it said so succinctly and with such intensity, power, prophetic life, agony, and beauty, that Jesus quoted the words when he was on the cross—a lyric provided by his famous, kingly, psalm-writing progenitor.

Jesus and David understood something about God that apparently God wants us to catch on to as well: There is music in those tragic lines, and not just pretty words that can be put to a melody. It's the kind of inner music that moves and ranges within a person's soul outside speech and understanding, that has the capacity to touch those far reaches of self. And they were to be sung, as the introduction to the psalm reads, "For the director of music. To the tune of 'Doe of the Morning.'" A creature at daybreak, thirsty, hungry, anticipating. A beautiful melody, lonely, agonized, and sung to the accompaniment of a lone harp, an early version of a guitar, setting David's complaint, the great howl in him, to music. Music is not context. It is the mode of expression, the means of delivery between the spirit in a man and the spirit of God; it is, again, how God communicated with the great king, spirit to spirit, one "after" the other.

The following is a brief narrative, but a useful one. Two people drink an equivalent amount of alcohol. One says, "I got drunk." The other says, "I might have had one drink too many." Because of the careful arrangement of words, the second explanation softens the intensity of the act, implying that the person is perhaps not much of a drinker, and that they had too much to drink is of no consequence, something they can live with. It misleads, but gently. What if that person has a problem with alcohol and the narrative they have created is simply their way of protecting themselves from the ravages of opinion while they go on their merry way drinking to whatever excess they desire? Is the person lying to himself or herself? It clearly looks that way.

See how pliable, how elastic the story is, how we can shape our words to say whatever we want them to say in our defense? But what does all this have to do with faith? More than we may want it to, perhaps. Scripture says, "Death and life are in the power of the tongue, and those who love it will eat its fruits" (Proverbs 18:21). Proverbs adds, "A gentle tongue is a tree of life" (Proverbs 15:4a). There are countless Scriptures that can help us understand not just the power of the tongue—power to heal, build, and encourage, or to destroy, break the spirit, and kill—but also its value when under the command of God. The King James Bible holds little back when discussing this troubling part of the body. "But the tongue no man can tame," it says. "It is an unruly evil, full of deadly poison" (James 3:8, KJV). To tame our tongue is to tame the world.

When we engage in something as simple as conversation, our words have life—the life we give them and the life behind or underneath the words, whether we are conscious of that meaning or not. Language is often, but not always, how the Holy Spirit calls us to himself. Sometimes that language makes no sound at all—a cup of water to the thirsty, taking care of an elderly person who has lost the ability to get along by themselves, countless acts of kindness that have led many to the Lord by service and by the love put into that service, however small or invisible. Language is the primary tool to communicate the goodness of the Lord, which doubtless has the power to change a life.

The flip side of that is just as true. Words can be used to seduce and mislead. Maybe you've heard the old phrase, "silver-tongued devil." It may sound a bit silly or old school, but it is a fairly good representation of how the devil operates. Words become snares, and those snares can be difficult to wriggle away from. The first order of defense is vigilance—continuous and well-informed.

> Dear friends, do not believe every spirit, but test the spirits to see whether they are from God, because many false prophets have gone out into the world.
>
> **1 John 4:1, NIV**

> It is the Spirit who gives life; the flesh is no help at all. The words that I have spoken to you are spirit and life.
>
> **John 6:63**

> Simon Peter answered him, "Lord to whom shall we go? You have the words of eternal life."
>
> **John 6:68**

I was never a big drinker. I'm not saying I didn't drink; it was just never a big part of my life. In college, I would have a drink at a club or fraternity mixer. I never liked beer and never had any alcohol in my apartment.

When I got married, I would order a drink when we went out to dinner. We did not keep any alcohol in the house for years. Eventually, we bought what we needed to make margaritas and mimosas. We kept a couple of bottles in our house.

After our divorce it was a different story. The narrative suffered some revision.

At first, it was a drink every other week or so. Later, it advanced to once a week. Then twice a week. The progression was slow but steady. Within two years' time, I could no longer tell who was in control, the drink or me. It had the makings of a classic country song, but the reasons behind it were deeper, more insidious, frighteningly precise, and I was the poor fool in its power. There came a time I knew I needed to address my drinking.

> *The Good Book's on the table and the liquor's in my glass*
> *I'd pray for forgiveness but I'm too ashamed to ask*
> *It's the bottle or the Bible, which one should I choose?*
> *If I could hear the voice of God, would I know what to do?*
>
> **—Randy Finchum, Kent Maxson, Jordan Mogey, "Spirits"**

It should be no surprise that alcohol is often referred to as "spirits." A sign above a liquor store might say "Wine and Spirits." Drinking became a thing. Though it didn't appear out of nowhere or happen in a vacuum, another narrative began to take shape under its power. There are many spirits we might follow—alcohol, drugs, sex, money, power, anger, despair, insecurity, or approval—and we often surrender authorship (and good sense) to the narratives they inspire, most of them unhealthy or in the service of another god.

Habits are made of stuff we like. We smoke because we like it. We do drugs, we steal, we philander or use foul language because of how it makes us feel, the relief it brings, or the illusion of relief. We become attached, drawn to its power like a moth to a flame. I was the feather; it was the wind. I surrendered my power to something that could harm me, that had command over me. The list of complicated psychologies that put the drink in my hand in the first place was bigger than I thought—depression, grief over the divorce, grief over the failure a marriage had become, and so on.

Recovery starts with recognition, that first spark of awareness that something is terribly wrong. It starts with becoming aware of the true enemy, even when that enemy is yourself. Too often it means hitting rock bottom, or somewhere close. Desperation, however, is not the enemy we think it is—any more than a call for help always signals weakness. I cannot conquer a spirit, one that is stronger, smarter, older, more desperate, and more cunning than me, simply by telling myself I can. It doesn't work like that. I cannot wrestle such an opponent alone and expect positive results. And the defeat that often follows any such attempt may just invite me back to the medication that made me a slave in the first place. It is a vicious cycle. All that to say that I cannot, of my own strength, overpower my demons. The road to recovery, the road to being me again, begins with recognition, with clarity in the heart.

> For I do not understand my own actions. For I do not do what I want, but I do the very thing I hate.
>
> **Romans 7:15**

The pain and the helplessness of my sin convinced me I was lost, that there was no hope for me. Even so, like those narratives I have attempted to explain, a prayer began to take shape in me, in my deepest heart. And only a lyric could flush it out.

> *I want to go to heaven 'cause hell is where I've been*
> *Matthew, Mark, Luke, and John mixed with Gordon's Gin*

I'm searching for salvation, to feel the Holy Ghost within

So fill me up with Spirits and wash away, wash away my sin

AUTHOR AND FINISHER

Clarity, when it comes—and it will come if you remain diligent and focused—can help you sort out all the many weights that burden you, help you name them, and call them out one by one. Clarity doesn't come cheap. But when the light comes on, it is a beautiful thing.

> So I find it to be a law that when I want to do right, evil lies close at hand. For I delight in the law of God, in my inner being, but I see in my members another law waging war against the law of my mind and making me captive to the law of sin that dwells in my members. Wretched man that I am! Who will deliver me from this body of death?
>
> **Romans 7:21–24**

I kept choosing to follow a spirit I despised because it provided me with a temporary yet false relief from pain. Because I did this, I ended up doubting the love and power of the Holy Spirit, who was always ready to offer me forgiveness. I am a sinner. I don't like this fact about myself, nor will it change dramatically on this side of heaven, but I am. I even asked myself, "How can I be forgiven by God when I keep failing? How can he possibly forgive me . . . again?" I don't know how, and like many of you I allowed doubt and disbelief to set their traps for me. And the truth is, this knowledge is over my head. It's too much for me. "Such knowledge is too wonderful for me, too lofty for me to attain" (Psalm 139:6, NIV).

No Way Out But Through

I can't tell you how I know or how it works, but I can tell you, and with some certainty, that God does forgive, and that it does work. Forgiveness, with its deep medicines, cleanses and clarifies us. God changes you. He did me—and is continuing to. That is my new narrative, the one I am still living, still co-editing, the one that is writing me. Like a book written by a skilled writer, a good draft deserves its share of revision and polish, the occasional edit here and there. He is, after all, the author and finisher. It makes for a better book, or, in this case, a better life, a better story, a better me.

Thanks be to God through Jesus Christ our Lord! So then, I myself serve the law of God with my mind, but with my flesh I serve the law of sin.

Romans 7:25

For I know the plans I have for you, declares the LORD, plans for welfare and not for evil, to give you a future and a hope.

Jeremiah 29:11

Fear not, little flock, for it is your Father's good pleasure to give you the kingdom.

Luke 12:32

In him, I am an individual, the best and truest version of myself. I will continue to grow, to change, to go from glory to glory by his design. That uniqueness, that individual he has created and is creating me to be, is not diminished among his people. I do not disappear or fade into the back-ground. If God is in me and God is in you, if God is in the stranger, and if I place myself in the midst of all of you, I become more than I am. The world, in that moment, becomes more than it is. It is a blessed household.

There is a long, beautiful, timeless, and tragic narrative associated with the word "Christ." He is the anointed son of David, the promised of God who came to save his people. That's you and me. As I struggle with my sins, I must never let the Evil One separate me from my Savior. I must not lose sight of why Jesus died on the cross. He died because I struggle with alcohol. He died because I struggle with pride. He died because I cannot, by my own reason or strength, live a good life or even have any idea what that is. I am a sinner. I am hardwired to sin, or at least by appearances (and those appearances are persuasive). On my own, I cannot break free of sin. I need a Savior. I will not let the Evil One tell me I am unlovable to God. (Repeat that to yourself often. Print it on your soul.) Pain teaches us to search out the narratives behind it, the ones that reinforce it. When we have an idea what is at the root of our pain, we are that much closer to claiming victory over it. Our narrative can be rewritten, with a happier, truer ending. None of this is possible, of course, without Christ. Pain teaches us to make better choices. To feel oneself aloof or detached from the whole can distort the narrative you were meant to enjoy and cultivate.

I was born cross-eyed. My parents attributed my clumsiness (always running into coffee tables, falling down the stairs, and tripping over things) to this condition. One day a friend of my mother's was at our house. She was a smoker. Between puffs, she would place her cigarette in the ashtray. I must have smelled the smoke from her cigarette because I put my face in the ashtray and burned my nose. My mother decided at that moment that maybe there was something more than my being cross-eyed that was wrong with my eyesight. Sure enough, when I was tested, the diagnosis was that I was extremely near-sighted. Soon I was wearing glasses that were about half an inch thick. My world looked different from that moment on. So did I.

When I look back on the many mistakes I have made in life, it becomes clear how my mistakes caused pain for myself and for others. Not unlike my childhood eyesight, my vision was at fault. Though not completely blind, I was running into things. But that pain led to awareness, and awareness gave me the opportunity to change.

Life is a continual series of choices. Faulty and uncorrected vision, not unlike bad choices we make, lead to pain. Pain takes us to the end of ourselves, or somewhere near it. But it can also lead to recognition, and recognition to awareness. Awareness leads to enlightenment, and enlightenment leads to strategies for positive change. Next comes recovery. All roads lead to Christ, who was monitoring this succession all along.

Devotional writer and mystic, Thomas Merton, speaking to a classroom of novices at a monastery, was once asked, "Does God do all the work of redemption?" Merton's answer was a simple and authoritative *yes*. "God does 100 percent of the work," he said. He then added, "But we do 100 percent of the work as well." The math doesn't work on paper, but that is how redemption and recovery work. It is more of a cooperation with and through the power of the Holy Spirit. Is it a mystery? Of course, it is. Can I explain it? No. I will give Scripture the last word.

> For we do not wrestle against flesh and blood, but against the rulers, against the authorities, against the cosmic powers over this present darkness, against the spiritual forces of evil in the heavenly places.
>
> **Ephesians 6:12**

SPIRITS

Randy Finchum, Kent Maxson, Jordan Mogey

The good book's on the table and the liquor's in my glass
I'd pray for forgiveness but I'm too ashamed to ask
It's the bottle or the Bible, which one should I choose?
If I could hear the voice of God, would I know what to do?

CHORUS

I want to go to heaven 'cause hell is where I've been
Matthew, Mark, Luke, and John mixed with Gordon's Gin
I'm searching for salvation, to feel the Holy Ghost within
So fill me up with Spirits and wash away, wash away my sins

The bottle whispers to me "Come on and take a sip
Your pain will all be over once I pass your lips"
And somewhere in these pages, I'm told, the answers there
But after all the things I've done can, he hear my prayers?

CHORUS

I want to go to heaven 'cause hell is where I've been
Matthew, Mark, Luke, and John mixed with Gordon's Gin
I'm searching for salvation, to feel the Holy Ghost within
So fill me up with Spirits and wash away, wash away my sins

BRIDGE

Is it faith, hope, and love or a drink to ease the pain
Do I reach out to Jesus or give into the devil again?

No Way Out But Through

Chapter 6

Forgiveness Has a
Soft Voice and a Tender Heart

It's not the lack of love that kills it in the end

No, it's refusing to forgive

Kent Maxson and Alyssa Trahan, "Forgiveness"

Forgiveness is the key to a prison of our own making. While that may sound like a line from a song (and would probably make a good one), I have seen and experienced it for myself. A form of slavery that takes concentrated effort to escape, unforgiveness binds both parties in the same pair of shackles. Earlier I mentioned that for some issues of life, particularly those deeper issues of the heart, only a song or line of poetry can come close to saying what can and needs to be said, especially the impossible things, those things for which words are scarce and hard to come by. While I believe that to be true, forgiveness requires but a few simple words. It doesn't need flowers, a poem, or a song, only courage and a willing heart. By holding on to an offense, you bind yourself to an unhealthy and miserable existence—a form of hard time.

We hear story after tragic story of family members and some ugly thing suspended in the midst of them—brother against brother, an estrangement of daughter and father, father and son, and so on. Sadly, the combinations are limitless. Much has been written on the subject. Googling *forgiveness* will get you a flood of responses, but as well-written, moving, and wise as those words may be, to forgive someone or to ask for someone's forgiveness takes an act of will—deliberate, intentional, given with a whole heart. It is, in essence, an act of surrender. I am no expert on the subject, but I can share from my experience, beginning with one of my songs.

> *You're gonna see what you want to see*
> *You're gonna believe what you want to believe*
> *And it's a hard thing to do but you have to choose,*
> *To let it go, or keep holding on*
> *Because love can't live without forgiveness*

Asking someone to forgive an offense is to first admit fault, which is never easy. To admit my guilt, my part of an argument or any offense that has remained unaddressed and had time to fester, touches me in the tenderest of places—my pride. Is it sticky? Of course, it is sticky. That is why we too often leave an offense unattended. Best to part company than further assault our pride. Tensions growl, then snap. We break old bonds. We divorce. We go our separate ways. We bury the thing as deep as conscience will allow and are foolish enough to think it will remain quiet. We create narratives to soothe the pain, but they are rarely true or effective. They work temporarily, if at all, and in patches, providing self-medication of the shallowest kind. We know that is the case, and we do it anyway.

To ask forgiveness is to allow mercy a chance to show itself, to allow its deep medicines to work. The desire to ask for forgiveness is usually the result of clarity—that moment when the bigger picture comes into view, pressed as you are with a lack of peace and rest, desperate for the words that would liberate you, that need to be said. Whether you are forgiven by the other person is not in your power. What *is* in your power is the contrition, the surrender, the silencing of pride, the humility—all in the service of mercy, justice, and ultimately love. To put forgiveness out front, whether asking for it or giving it, is to act according to the counsel of Scripture.

To ask forgiveness is to cooperate with the bigger picture. If it takes time, and it will, it is only right and just. The beautiful thing is that both parties are altered, not with some form of street wisdom that makes them wary of any dealing with you or me, but with freedom that touches both parties and may salvage a friendship. And if the other party refuses you, if they scorn you, look to Christ himself for wisdom and the strength to stand, remaining consistent in what power you have. Place forgiveness out front and trust it to teach you how to act, what to do and say.

Forgiveness and the mercies it will ask of you are the path to knowing the deeper rule of love, the rule that governs and sweetens it. What is it about forgiving someone that is so difficult? Or about forgiving yourself? Sweeping it all under the metaphorical rug doesn't help, though we are all guilty of it. The hard truth is that forgiveness is a choice—one that starts and ends with love.

We must develop and maintain the capacity to forgive. He who
is devoid of the power to forgive is devoid of the power to love.

Martin Luther King Jr.

No Way Out But Through

LOVE IS NOT LOVE WITHOUT IT

When I was in sixth grade at Rusk Elementary School in Midland, Texas, my teacher was Mrs. Harvick. From her I learned the fundamentals of reading, writing, and arithmetic. My memories of those times may not always be clear, but there was one thing that was a staple in her class that I remember vividly, an activity she conducted regularly, that was important to her: memorizing and reciting literature.

Mrs. Harvick would take a famous poem, speech, historical document, or any other piece of literature and hand it out to the class. She would then assign each of us one line from the handout to memorize. In a loud voice she would call out the name of a poem, "The Jabberwocky," for instance, by Lewis Carroll. Our task was to commit the assigned passage, a single line, to memory and then recite it without flaw on command. We never knew when this recitation might happen. It could begin while we were at our desk drawing, or it could be while we were working on a math problem. In other words, we were wise to learn it quickly and succinctly. As we continued our work, the person who had the first line would announce the title of the chosen text and begin. One by one, and in loud voices, we would recite our given line in the correct order. Fearful of missing our cue, we had to listen carefully in order to know when it was time to speak. It was an effective teaching tool.

As annoying as it may have been, this drill taught us to listen carefully and to be vigilant. Over time, we discovered that we not only knew our lines but that most of us had also committed the entire poem to memory. But out of all the literature we memorized, the passage I remember most, and can recite every word of to this day, is 1 Corinthians 13, written by the apostle Paul. Known by many as "the Love Chapter," I have read multiple translations of these verses, and most every time I learn something new. Every version seems to capture a fresh nuance and understanding of the complex subject of love. I have included it here.

If I speak in the tongues of men or of angels, but have not love, I am only a resounding gong or a clanging cymbal. If I have the gift of prophecy and can fathom all mysteries and all knowledge, and if I have a faith that can move mountains, but do not have love, I am nothing. If I give all I possess to the poor and give over my body to hardship that I may boast, but do not have love, I am nothing.

Love is patient, love is kind. It does not envy, it does not boast, it is not proud. It does not dishonor others, it is not self-seeking, it is not easily angered, it keeps no record of wrongs. Love does not delight in evil but rejoices with the truth. It always protects, always trusts, always hopes, always perseveres.

Love never fails. But where there are prophecies, they will cease; where there are tongues, they will be stilled; where there is knowledge, it will pass away. For we know in part and we prophesy in part, but when completeness comes, what is in part disappears. When I was a child, I talked like a child, I thought like a child, I reasoned like a child. When I became a man, I put the ways of childhood behind me. For now we see only a reflection as in a mirror; then we shall see face to face. Now I know in part; then I shall know fully, even as I am fully known.

And now these three remain: faith, hope and love. But the greatest of these is love.

1 Corinthians 13, NIV

It is difficult to imagine words like that not leaving an imprint, binding themselves in some unknown way to that part of us that thinks, examines, processes, chooses, shows mercy, forgives, and, of course, loves.

Forgiveness, like love, clears the heart of the unnecessary and allows us to look deeper into ourselves, not in a self-absorbed, what's-in-it-for-me kind of way, but in glimpses of what God sees in us, what only love can possibly see. Forgiveness strips away harshness and complaint, often effecting an inexplicable calm. Love is not love without it.

As suggested in the beginning of this chapter, unforgiveness is a locked door or cell, one that holds both parties captive, the offender and the offended. Both suffer under the penalty of unforgiveness, and the only possible medication, is love. And while love and forgiveness are not the same thing, they share a likeness. Following the cues from the "Love Chapter," can we not say that forgiveness is patient? I have been there enough times to think it must be. Forgiveness is also kind. It is not proud, rude, or self-seeking. Such things defeat the purpose. If I say that love has a soft voice and a tender heart, can I not say the same about forgiveness? Love and forgiveness thrive together. It was for forgiveness that Christ demonstrated his great love, that we might know the forgiveness of God and know it intimately, and that we might offer forgiveness (and the mercy that seasons it) to others and to ourselves.

> This is my blood of the covenant, which is poured out for many
> for the forgiveness of sins.
>
> **Matthew 26:28, NIV**

The record keepers, those who record and take to heart every offense, however slight, do not realize how they strangle and undermine their peace. With the recording of each offense, they gather another weight upon themselves, and with so much gravity they can hardly move forward. Love means letting go of an offense. It may be the hardest thing you will ever do, but the joy and freedom that follows is greater than the intensity with which you held on to it. Freedom is the ultimate point. "It was for freedom that Christ has set us free" (Galatians 5:1, NASB1995). The word *paradise* παραδεισος [*paradeisos*], in one sense, means a park, "a place of pleasure, shady and well-watered, a place where freedom is freest, where innocence is its best self." If love is paradise present—and I am convinced that it is—others will see it in you and catch on. Love is contagious that way.

Love is a shield that protects you from offense. It is not possible to offend someone who abides in the love of Christ. As contradictory as this will sound, I cannot be hurt in love. The nails penetrated the flesh of Christ but had no effect on his love. On the contrary, his love was made clearer, truer, deeper, more pronounced when put to the extreme test. If I take that bullet to protect my child, the bullet cannot harm me. Love sees to that. Even if I lose my life, I have given it without the slightest reservation—for my child, my spouse, my friend. Jesus did it for the stranger.

To seek forgiveness and to forgive is itself a great trust, a trust in the rule of God, the rule of love itself. It is a trust given. Forgiveness has a life of its own, and when that life is honored, when one rests within its care and protections, it behaves like love, with all the benefits mentioned in 1 Corinthians 13. I forgive by faith, the faith I live by, and that forgiveness alters me. It requires a step of faith, and just as often the leap, but love empowers it, adding all its protections and the tranquility it is known by. I rest in the hope of God's wisdom, of which forgiveness is among its highest strains.

If I use the word *forgiveness* and *love* interchangeably, it is not altogether accidental. Because of their fluid character, one becomes indistinguishable at times from the other. Where there is forgiveness, love is the life behind it, even as it is the ground beneath. One of the few absolutes you will encounter in this life, in spite of our mismanagement or misunderstanding of it, is that love never fails. It never falters, stumbles, or hesitates. Even at the appearance of failure, when someone scorns your attempt at reconciliation, love holds fast. It does not waver or lose strength. It digs in deeper. It opens you up in a sense, clarifies things.

> *You're gonna see what you want to see*
> *You're gonna believe what you want to believe*
> *And it's a hard thing to do but you have to choose*
> *To let it go, or keep holding on*
> *Because love can't live without forgiveness*

WHO CHOOSETH ME

To forgive is to place a higher value on the law of love than on that which feeds your pride, a higher value on the relationship than on yourself. Relationships are not always easy. Forgiveness, like love itself, will cost you something. This is where so many of us fall short of genuine forgiveness or faith—it costs too much. Jesus told us exactly what it would cost when he said, "If anyone would come after me, let him deny himself and take up his cross and follow me" (Matthew 16:24). In *The Merchant of Venice*, Shakespeare says something very similar. The lovestruck Bassanio faces a choice among three small chests, one of which has the image of his beloved Portia. If he chooses the right chest, the one with her picture inside, he gets to marry her. The first chest is made of pure gold with an inscription that reads, "Who chooseth me attains what many men desire" (2.7.5) The second is sterling silver. Its inscription reads, "Who chooseth me shall get as much as he deserves" (2.7.7). The last and least of the three chests is made of base lead. The inscription warns, "Who chooseth me must give and hazard all he hath" (2.7.9). By the wisdom and rule of love, Bassanio chooses the least of the three, the lead chest. Jesus could have used those exact words and not missed a beat: "Who chooseth me must give and hazard all he hath." And who says Shakespeare has nothing more to teach?

The passage directly following 1 Corinthians 13:13 says to "follow the way of love" (1 Corinthians 14:1, NIV). Like love or redemption, forgiveness is not a one-time event or decision. It is a daily, hourly, moment-by-moment enterprise. As cliché as this may sound, forgiveness, like love, is a way of life, a thing maintained by proper care and continuous exercise. Love sets life to music.

What do I gain by holding a grudge?

Bondage.

Frustration.

Annoyance.

Smallness.

Confusion.

Distance from God.

Distance from peace.

Distance from self.

By holding a grudge, I give another person power over my life. I give the dark and ugly thing between us power over me, over my thought life, my actions, my words, putting restraints on mercy. Again, there is but one trustworthy medication, and there is none so sweet.

> A new commandment I give to you, that you love one another:
> just as I have loved you, you also are to love one another.
> **John 13:34**

There are people I love who have chosen to eliminate me from their life. I cannot put into words how helpless it makes me feel when all that exists between us is silence and rejection. At this point, I have little choice but to surrender this weight to God, for I cannot carry it. But I can love them with a whole heart. I can forgive myself and I can pray for them, with sincerity and good hope, whether we are ever reconciled or not. Forgiveness, among the other gifts God has given me, allows the freedom to live my life by his design. When I make a daily decision to forgive, I can go on about my business, confident that I am doing my part, doing what I can, doing whatever is asked of me, responding to the law of Christ and of my Father in heaven. I am no longer a captive. Forgetting an offense won't be easy. God may drown an offense in the depths of the sea, but I am not that smart or powerful. All I can do is forgive and keep forgiveness out front, give it first voice, first seat of importance. I can nurture it with prayer. I can allow it to shape and purify my decisions and my thought life. I can make it watchman over the affairs of my heart. An attitude of forgiveness may just overpower the memory of an offense.

As he was dying, suffering impossible torment, among his last words Jesus said, "Father forgive them, for they know not what they do" (Luke 23:34). When brutally offended, when stripped of everything, of life itself, it is godly to forgive. It may be the greatest test of faith of who we are as Christians. We may have to grit our teeth at times. It may be a sheer act of duty or obedience, but that same duty and obedience offered to God is transformed into joy and liberty. Allow its counsel to shape your decisions. Live free under its guidance. As Christ did, allow forgiveness to have the last word, remembering always that love is not love without it.

FORGIVENESS

Kent Maxson, Alyssa Trahan

Harsh words, slammed door, broken glass on the floor

Both sides are keeping score

Another big fight, another cold, cold night

Separated by their need to be right

When no one's giving in

Don't you know that no one's gonna win

CHORUS

You're gonna see what you want to see

You're gonna believe what you want to believe

And it's a hard thing to do, but you have to choose

To let it go or keep holding on

Because love can't live without forgiveness

One bed, two sides, no one can apologize.

Being held back by their pride

They just can't get along, but both agree the other's wrong

If they keep letting this go on

They'll never make it through

Oh, and all they're gonna do is lose

BRIDGE

It's not the lack of love that kills it in the end

No, it's refusing to forgive

CHORUS

You're gonna see what you want to see

You're gonna believe what you want to believe

And it's a hard thing to do, but you have to choose

To let it go or keep holding on

Because love can't live without forgiveness

Chapter 7
Some of Us Get a Dog

It is not good that the man should be alone.

Genesis 2:18

There is a difference between being alone and being lonely. One is more tolerable than the other. Most of us are alone much of the time, day or night—in our cars, at home, at our desks, cutting the grass, brushing our teeth, walking to school, doing our homework, or writing a poem—or a song. Not only is it common and natural, it is necessary for stable emotional and spiritual health. Even Jesus withdrew on occasion and found something in solitude that was necessary. It would be creepy to have someone with us at *all* times. We grow out of that condition very early in life. Either way, we balance being alone with time spent in the society of others—family, a neighbor, friends, a spouse, people at work, or at church, and so on. Some of us get a dog.

Being lonely is a different issue. It demands a little more from us than merely being alone. Where being alone is the mere absence of others, loneliness is a condition that brings that absence into sharp distinction, at times to our discomfort. Having no one for company but ourselves, for some, becomes intolerable. The extremes of any emotional state can become toxic. Depending on the severity, one might hear the voice of his or her conscience (or an uneasy inner monologue) say something like, "See, nobody wants to be around you," or "Aha, I told you so." This is mere imagination, narratives that our militant extremes fashion in us, but they can be persuasive. They can also be difficult to circumnavigate or silence.

Then there are existential questions that ask some form of, "Am I really here?" These questions can be particularly nasty. One looks upon a clear night sky with all its beauty and spectacle only to turn sour with, "Of all the billions of stars and galaxies out there, what or who in the heck am I? What am I to think when Shakespeare and Kansas, two principal authorities on human nature, say I am nothing but dust?" *All we are is dust in the wind . . .*

Think of a man or woman in solitary confinement. It is difficult to imagine a lonelier existence, or a more troubling one—bleak, nothing but gray walls and silence. To summarize what we all know and have had some experience with, being alone is normal, common, even necessary. Loneliness is an emotional state brought on by separation from others, voluntarily or involuntarily. At its mildest, it undermines comfort. At its extremes, it is, or can be, crippling.

Opinions about solitude go back to the first pages of the Bible, and they are not all good. It is one of the most primitive issues of man's existence and, unmistakably, of his well-being. The first mention of anything in Scripture that was "not good" had to do with solitude. God himself said so. The work he had accomplished on day one was good; days two, three, and so on—all good. Evening and morning were the first day, the second, the third, and so on. Remember, God himself was not alone. "Let us make man in *our* image," he said, "after *our* likeness" (Genesis 1:26a). But the man is alone. In short time, he realizes he is alone. He suffers an ache he cannot name, unfamiliar to all creation. And even God admits this can't be good.

And the LORD God said, It is not good that the man should be alone.

Genesis 2:18a, KJV

Scripture says that "The LORD God planted a garden eastward in Eden; and there he put the man whom he had formed" (Genesis 2:8, KJV). Eden was created for man. The whole purpose was fellowship with God. One on one. This was all good because all that God does is good. And it worked— for a season. That it was or suddenly became "not good" is a twist in the narrative. Is it a condition God did not foresee or expect? What baffles me is that according to the narrative, at least superficially, God himself wasn't enough. Even as I write, that feels impossible to imagine. How can God, the creator of the universe, the Alpha and Omega, the beginning and the end, who created paradise (literal and metaphorical) for man, who first breathed life into man—how could he not fill the empty space that Adam's solitude had awakened? Now *that* is a question.

We talk and sermonize with grand speeches about Adam in the garden. We color the story with bright foliage—green, abundant, lush, sunlight sparkling on the dew, without corruption or even the possibility of corruption or age, perhaps predating time itself, the animals at ease with man and each other, Adam walking with God in the cool of the day, speaking to him as one speaks to a friend. All is bliss. All is unity and solidarity. You get the picture: The idyll glows in a beatific mist. It seems almost heretical to think that all that somehow wasn't enough, that God looked on man and saw the unease within him and said, "Wait a minute. This can't be good."

Adam began to notice that all the animals had a counterpart, a mate, an *other* who was like them and not like them, whom they could couple with and reproduce after their own kind. He had no such being. Unlike every male animal that roamed the garden, Adam had only himself. He could not reproduce after his own kind. Though he was made in the likeness of his Maker, he was not like his Maker. Something was missing—or someone. It certainly was for Adam. At last, God provided medication for man's "aloneness" and formed the woman out of man to be his *other*, his helper, his companion, the mother of his children, his comfort, his ally in thought and action, the watcher of his metaphorical back, and, best of all, the good medicine to his loneliness (loneliness being a condition we have just noted was "not good").

We all know the story, how things went south sometime after that, how the couple was banished from the garden. But before blaming anyone for anything and igniting an old argument, the greater point is this: The ultimate rightness (or "righteousness") of a man or a woman is to walk with God, to know his thoughts and to follow those thoughts the best one can, to know his every movement, however subtle, with a vigilance and pursuit that becomes the first order of life, continuous, without end or repentance.

The need for connection is primal in us. You and I were made for fellowship, to flourish in the company and society of others with God in the midst of us. There is a measure of incompleteness without it. In the beginning, that fellowship was with God alone. Springing from that fellowship was fellowship with others. This seems to be the pattern established from the beginning. Three out of the four Gospels essentially agree that loving God is bound to loving your neighbor. Of all the lessons this book could possibly teach, this one is central, of the first order: loving God is bound to loving your neighbor. I will say more about it presently, but in loving my neighbor, I am, in a very real sense, loving God in obedience to his great command. Every other Christian enterprise pales against these two commands.

ALONE WITH GOD

Here is a question for you: If God is everywhere at once, how can he be alone with you? I am not sure you or I have an answer for that, or are capable of one, so here's a more sensible question: What does it mean to be alone with God? Can you be alone with him in traffic? Can you be alone with him in a crowd? Is he in a church building? Do I need to go to a secluded place in nature to be isolated with the Almighty? The short answer is that to be alone with God is all of the above. It is possible to be alone with an omnipresent God anywhere, anytime, and under any condition we can imagine—through the tedium of our workday, on a stroll through the neighborhood, driving down the road, whether I am angry, sad, or happy. You get the idea. *Omnipresent* means present everywhere all the time, so the possibilities are limitless.

> Now when Jesus heard this, he withdrew from there in a boat to a desolate place by himself.
>
> **Mathew 14:13**

At the beheading of John the Baptist, it is not difficult to imagine that Jesus was so overwhelmed with grief and other conflicting thoughts that he needed to be physically alone. Perhaps he needed to separate himself from the distraction of others, to be alone with his thoughts, to be alone with God. Either way, he was alone, but he wasn't lonely. He may have suffered emotional pain, but he was not abandoned or alone in his suffering. Having practiced the presence of God all his life, he walked in that confidence. As mentioned earlier, being physically alone is natural and common. In fact, it can be very healing. What is difficult to deal with is being alone emotionally or spiritually. Jesus sought a connection with God to deal with his pain over the loss of John the Baptist, the prophet who had announced him to the world.

There is a small, protected area in Nashville called Radnor Lake State Park. It is my sanctuary. When I am struggling in any area of my life, I often go there and walk by myself to be alone with my thoughts and with God. There almost always are other people walking the trails, but they are not with me. I am physically alone, just me and my thoughts. I pass people occasionally and will sometimes nod my head or say hi, but I am alone. I go to Radnor for that specific purpose—to connect both emotionally and spiritually with God. I have a true and worthy companion in him.

I know people who say they have heard the audible voice of God. I would love to be able to say that, but I cannot. He does not speak to me in an audible way. Or maybe he does and I don't recognize it. I don't know. But I do at times experience him in a fleeting thought that seems to come from out of nowhere. It might be in a wisp of wind, a rustling in the leaves, the flight of a hawk, or a small critter scampering across the trail. Some would say this is my imagination, attaching meaning to random events. That may be true, but these random moments have often led me to answers I had fervently sought for some time. Not to mention that according to Scripture, the kingdom of God is within you (Luke 17:21), which opens whole new possibilities.

God will speak to me and reveal himself to me how he pleases. If audible, then audible. If in silence, in silence. He knows how I am tuned. From childhood we learn that every snowflake has a different pattern from the next. As baffling as that is, it helps me understand this aspect of God's character. His relationship to me is unique, unlike anyone else's in the world. Even the word *unique* doesn't quite say it. To be fashioned and shaped in his image is to be like no one but myself, as he envisioned me in the first place.

Sometimes we want and need to be physically alone in order to recharge. You can, however, be physically alone or isolated and experience pain because of the longing for connection. The connection you long for might be physical, but most of the time, it is emotional connection you desire. Today we are offered ways to connect with others that could hardly be imagined even a generation ago. Social media provides all the props of connection. It thrives and hums with busyness, and we believe it to be authentic: "I am never alone. I have Facebook. I have Twitter (now X). I have Instagram." Blah. Blah. Blah. Those are but alternatives to genuine relationship. The sad thing is, we all know it, and we don't seem to care. We act as if each social media venue is true, that it is exactly what it says it is. And it works. It has revolutionized culture. But for good? I am not sure I have an answer. It is the stuff addictions are made of. It is a kind of heroine I think we could do without. The industry has made a few folks very wealthy because of its powerful charm (and the algorithms that rule over us). Relationships are shallow, and yet, again, we don't care because shallow is what we've become used to. It is what we have. It may be that we simply like the distance. It is safe. Conversation is indirect, and I can cut someone off with a mere swipe.

I have a neighbor, a man who lives next door to me, but I don't know him. The Bible tells me to love my neighbor, but I can't really say that I do. If I do not know my neighbor, how can I love him? Even as I write, the question unsettles me. According to Scripture, it is not really a choice to love or not love our neighbor. It is a command.

> "Teacher, which is the greatest commandment in the Law?" Jesus replied, 'Love the Lord your God with all your heart and with all your soul and with all your mind. This is the first and greatest commandment. And the second is like it. Love your neighbor as yourself.'
>
> **Matthew 22:36–39, NIV**

This passage only pretends to be two commandments. The first and great commandment, Jesus said, was to love God with all your heart, soul, and mind. The second commandment, however, is like it, which, we could say, is equal to it. One mirrors the other (Matthew 22:39, Mark 12:31,

No Way Out But Through

Luke 10:27). It is not a stretch to suggest that to love your neighbor is, in the eyes and opinion and economy of Jesus, the same as loving God himself. In other words, to fulfill the second commandment is to fulfill the first. And the first means little or nothing without the second. They are inextricably bound, even as a single command.

Here's another head-exploder: If my neighbor is a believer, if he or she has Jesus in their heart and it is my desire as a believer to fellowship with Jesus, then I have to make inroads into my neighbor's heart, if but to meet with Jesus there. If the kingdom of Heaven is within them, it is the same. I have to make a significant investment in their lives for their ultimate good, that I may know the God that abides there, that awaits my company.

This type of awareness, this kind of understanding of Scripture has the potential to change the game entirely. We go to church. We sing. We praise God. We pray. On and on. You get the message. We do a thousand things to worship God. But according to the words of Jesus above, if I do not love my neighbor (essentially anyone who comes into my path, not just the person who lives next door), all that effort is reduced to nothing.

Religion has taken the place of the real work of the gospel. Religion is easy. Anyone can sing. Anyone can read the Bible, put a few dollars in the plate, sit in a Sunday School class, argue doctrine and feel good about themselves. So what? If that struggling single mother in your congregation leaves that building without help, without *your* help, what good has all your effort achieved? "Yeah, but we sang songs to Jesus!" It is empty air as long as that child two rows down is threatened with hunger because mom's three jobs won't cut it.

Enough. It's getting warm in here. I am as convicted as you are.

In life, you and I are going to be alone. You are going to be abandoned, left to your own devices and supply. You are going to be scorned. Any adult will be able to say the same. But to read the verses above as we have expanded them here, means that we are never to be alone. If I want to love God, I will seek those within my reach, those whom I can love and comfort and assist and listen to and offer acts of kindness, however small. It begs the question, "How can I possibly be lonely if I love God, if I believe his Word, if I believe that to love him with all my heart, soul, and mind is to love my neighbor with that same heart, soul, and mind, and in the same strength?"

All this puts being alone or being lonely in the truest and most promising perspective. Even so, you and I have a choice. We can obey his commandment—for in God that commandment is singular (loving God and loving your neighbor)—and by doing so, live according to a higher life with all the promises of heaven. Or you can choose to make an idol of emotional pain caused by loneliness and be led away from the only true source of love and all its divine medicines. I think the former is the better choice.

ALONE

Kent Maxson, Jordan Mogey, and Alyssa Trahan

There was a time I thought we had it all
But we were so naive and way too young
There's no way we could have known where it was gonna lead
And it's only looking back that I can see

CHORUS

The most alone I've ever been was when I was with you
Side by side but miles apart, we didn't want to face the truth
Empty touch and hollow words and walls we couldn't break
through
Oh, the most alone I've ever been
was when I was with you.

It's amazing just how much you can love someone
Then deny it as you watch it come undone
And I've heard silence say more than a single word
I've been numb and thinking I'd rather feel the hurt

CHORUS

The most alone I've ever been was when I was with you
Side by side but miles apart, we didn't want to face the truth
Empty touch and hollow words and walls we couldn't break
through
Oh, the most alone I've ever been
was when I was with you.

BRIDGE

Now I've got a love that showed me how it should be

And maybe it was my fault, but honestly

CHORUS

The most alone I've ever been was when I was with you

Side by side but miles apart, we didn't want to face the truth

Empty touch and hollow words and walls we couldn't break
through

Oh, the most alone I've ever been

Was when I was with you.

Chapter 8
I'm Just Me When I'm With You

Touch me, remind me who I am.

Stanley Kunitz, "Touch Me"

I lived at home with my parents my first year of college. It wasn't a problem most of the time, though my dad would often forget I was a grown man, or what I considered at the time to be a grown man. One weekend, he and Mom visited friends in Amarillo. Before leaving, he told me that while they were gone, I could invite some of my friends over. He even said we could have a few beers, but there were to be no parties. I was nineteen. The legal drinking age in Texas at that time was eighteen.

I was an obedient son (most of the time). I did as he asked and did not have a party. I invited three of my basketball teammates over, and we sat around talking. I wasn't much of a beer drinker even then, but my friends were. Between the three of them, they finished off a couple of six-packs. There was no music, no girls, no party. There were four guys sitting around the patio, talking and drinking beer. I am not sure how anyone could call that a party.

When my parents returned home, the house was clean and in order. Nothing was broken. There was no mess to clean up. Nothing was out of place. You would think this the end of the story, but not so for my dad. Having found some beer cans in the trash out in the alley, he was convinced I had thrown a party. Certain I had broken his rules, he grounded me. I was nineteen years old, in college, and was grounded for a week because three of my friends came over and drank beer. Everything I did was within his guidelines, but it didn't matter.

I was furious. Off and on through the years, I tried to convince him that I had not had a party and that only three of my friends came to the house. He never admitted he was wrong. There were times I felt he wanted to apologize and come clean, that he had made a mistake, but he never did. Suspended between us as it was, unresolved but aging and without any real bite, over time it became a toy between us, a joke that made us both laugh.

While writing this book, my father passed away. At ninety-two, he had lived a long life that I was blessed to be a part of for sixty-four years. He was a good man. Not perfect, but good. Which is kind of perfect. He had idiosyncrasies and, like the rest of us, he made some mistakes. He was not one to hand out a lot of praise. I think, in his mind, if you did what was expected of you, why should you be praised for it? It wasn't that he lacked pride in his children's accomplishments, he just expected you to excel at whatever you did, so he didn't always verbalize his feelings when you did succeed. He could also be stubborn, like his insistence that I had thrown a party, a thing he refused to let go of. He was more stubborn than I am, which isn't an easy thing to achieve. I suppose I am a lot like him.

You always knew where you stood with my dad. And he was consistent. His beliefs and behavior didn't change regardless of who his audience was. To him, if you were a Christian while at church, you should be a Christian anywhere else and in all areas of your life, public and private. As imperfect—that is, as human—as he was, he lived out his beliefs and to the high standards he was used to, whether in his marriage, his family, at work, at play, in his hobbies, or in his time alone. I never saw a hint of hypocrisy in my dad, and I kept a closer watch than anyone else. I can say without reservation he was authentic in everything he did.

In my entire life, I never heard my father say one curse word. I am not exaggerating. Not one. Foul language was just not his thing. The very worst I ever remember him saying was "dagnabbit." The fact that he never used profanity seems a small thing until you realize that he took his faith seriously. He was a follower of Jesus in every area of his life, not just when he was in the church building. He thought the use of profanity wrong. It didn't matter where you were, what was going on in your life, or if you smashed your thumb with a hammer, he had no taste or tolerance for foul language.

If Daddy was anything, he was authentic. It was his code, the rule he lived by.

The word *authentic* means that you are you who are, that there is no dissembling or counterfeiting self, whether in the society of others or alone. You are faithful to the core of who you are and what you believe. In spite of what the world may see in Christians as a group, or how many highly visible Christian leaders may prove to be frauds, authenticity was, is, and will remain one of the first and most essential traits of a follower of Jesus. As much as I value this quality, I have to constantly monitor myself. It is a rigid standard, and to maintain vigilance in it is a worthwhile practice. Am I the same person regardless of who I am with, where I am at, or what may be going on in my life at the time?

There are lots of possible reasons for a lack of authenticity, however mild or extreme, and acceptance may be the chief among them. Our insecurities direct us at times to project a less than true image of ourselves. We market ourselves to different groups for acceptance, to fit in. It is a form of branding, shaping our image to its most adaptable, most acceptable, and most attractive version. A *brand* is "a public image, reputation, or identity conceived of as something to be marketed or promoted." As a society we devote enormous amounts of energy to marketing and branding ourselves. The most successful brands market themselves around their core values. Social media venues have played their part. With YouTube, a camera, and a few props, anyone can create what amounts to their own TV show. We are so tuned as a culture to believe everything we see simply because it's on the screen. If well done, well managed, and well promoted, it is through such productions that stars are made. We've given these stars a name: influencers. It is a frightful word if you think about it in a spiritual context.

Authenticity is attractive. So all is done to create the appearance of it, which is one of the more delicious ironies—creating an appearance of authenticity or truth. But the image of the thing is not the thing itself.

If you were to hire a firm to help you establish your company's brand, they would ask several questions to determine what your brand is: "What do you stand for?" and "What are your core values?" Then they would help align everything in your company to adhere to those values and brand image. You would then have to consistently incorporate those agreed-upon values throughout your company in order to solidify your brand. But all of this would fall apart if the execution (or actions) of your company did not align with its message or statement of values.

If we take this idea of a corporate brand or philosophy and apply it to ourselves, we can learn a lot about who we are, what motivates us, and why. The issue then becomes whether our personal brand truly represents who we are. A company can advertise they have the "best customer service in the industry." But if you see one of their employees curse out a customer, you might lose faith in that company's image. In brand marketing, it is essential to be consistent with your values in order to create a lasting brand image. Anything that contradicts your professed values will expose you as a fraud. One slip-up can destroy your company.

If this holds true in the business world, does it not also hold true in your personal life? If you have a reputation for keeping your word, to keep your "brand" viable you must continue to keep your word.

I've got a satchel full of masks I wear out in the world
There's the one I wear to work and for talking to a girl
There's one for Sunday morning and there's one for the bar
It's easy to lose track of who you are

THE TEDIOUS WORK OF MASQUERADE

Do some of these words in brand marketing sound familiar when it comes to who you really are? Think about these words: *authentic, image, reputation, identity, representation, consistent.* If they apply to branding a company, how much more do they apply to me if I identify myself as a follower of Jesus? Shouldn't I be exuding the same traits no matter where I go or whom I am with? If foul language is something you would not use as a follower of Jesus when you are in a church building, shouldn't that same conviction apply to you in your workplace?

I have known people who led Sunday School classes and were full of "praise the Lord" messages on Sunday. On Monday, they were cursing at their employees for some mistake. I have sat in church and sung hymns of praise to God, then by the end of the week chewed out the serviceman at the car dealership because my car wasn't ready as promised. My dad would not be proud of me for this type of hypocrisy.

Please don't misunderstand me: We will all make mistakes. We are all human. We are sinners. Our mistakes are just further proof of our need for a Savior. Thankfully by the grace of God, we are forgiven. But mistakes should be the exceptions to our life brand, never the rule. If they are not the exception, then they *are* your "brand."

Earlier I mentioned the first and greatest commandment and the second which is like it: that you should love God with all your heart, soul, and mind, and love your neighbor as yourself. If these are the two greatest commandments, shouldn't they be the "brand" a follower of Jesus no matter where they are? I want to be the same person no matter where I am or what I am doing. This demands discipline, vigilance, and consistency.

> *I've got a satchel full of masks to wear out in the world*
> *There's the one I wear to work and for talking to a girl*
> *One for Sunday morning and one for the bar*
> *It's easy to lose track of who you are*

I was raised with three sisters. If you include mom and dad, it was an entire household who knew me better than anyone else on the planet. If I tried to put on airs or pretend I was something I am not, they would put me in my place on the spot. But they accepted me, all of me—the good, the bad, the small, the large. I can say the same of my wife Cindy in our household of two. Home is special to me for that reason: I don't have to wear myself out pretending I am someone or something I am not. Sustaining a lie is not easy; it takes a lot of energy to put on a show. It is exhausting. It is also dishonest.

In a business, a customer is the prize, someone who has been wooed, acquired, then groomed to believe in a product and, more importantly, to buy that product. For the individual, acceptance is the prize, approval of the tribe. When it is attained by deception, however slight, the acceptance is fraudulent, no matter how much excitement, attraction, or devotion it generates.

We have all been raised on spectacle. Some artists can fill a stadium or an arena with tens of thousands of screaming fans. We all know how it works, and we are easily led and sold. Spectacle is an industry, an industry with many years of study and practice doing one thing, creating spectacle—shiny objects, personalities that are larger than life, reality TV shows that we are convinced are true to life, all those lucky folks who are famous for being famous. As it is with professional wrestling, which is primarily a staged event, there is some part of us that knows it's fake—we just don't care. That "fakeness" is part of the charm. It entertains us, and what is more important than that? It is a momentary fix based on untruths, unrealities, and folks wearing elaborate masks. The energy required to keep up the facade is draining. Consciously or unconsciously, we are continually being trained in deception. It is a hidden rule of culture. There is no peace in it, or in anything like it.

Jesus, who alone is our peace, offers an alternative, a way back, a path to rest and comfort—a path to peace, glorious and true, everlasting and lifegiving. To each of us, he has said, "Come to me, all who labor and are heavy laden, and I will give you rest" (Matthew 11:28). In Christ, we can be ourselves at last, the truest version, stripped of all that was fabricated, all the myths we have created about ourselves—those we are aware of and those we are unconscious of. I am most myself when I am in Christ.

> *I'm just me when I'm with you*
> *What you see is what is true*
> *Exactly who I am as a person, as a man*
> *I'm just me when I'm with you*

Most of us have plenty of myths to spare. We often live by more of them than we'd like to admit. To come to Christ is to come to the waters. Metaphor aside, this is a powerful invitation, and it has two parts. One has to do with thirst. The other has to do with cleansing. We come because our thirst is of a nature so overwhelming that only a savior can possibly quench it.

> Come, all you who are thirsty, come to the waters; and you who have no money, come, buy and eat! Come, buy wine and milk without money and without cost.
>
> **Isaiah 55:1, NIV**

Secondly, it is by the waters of Christ that we are washed clean. When I come to Christ, not only are my physical and emotional needs met, but those things that trouble me, from crimes I have committed against others to the smallest unkindnesses, are washed away. All the grime and decay of so many years are cleansed and replaced with new thoughts, new hopes, new possibilities, and all-new dreams. How cool is that?

Being who we truly are brings tranquility and freedom from the tedious work of masquerade. Our personal brand will reflect this authenticity. Being genuine means there is no more pretending. We are who we are the fallen now forgiven, those who live and move and have their being in him who is the truth himself. As authenticity permeates every aspect of our lives, it influences the very sound of our words as we speak them, even the silence we offer as we listen to someone else's story. Authenticity brings with it powerful medicines, the first of which is its ability to grant permission to those around you to do the same—that is to discover, celebrate, and simply *be* themselves. Holiness itself is no more than being who you are, all possible counterfeits having been erased from the record.

If we live authentically, we are more equipped to detect the inauthentic in those around us. I was told by a friend that when someone is being trained to recognize counterfeit money, they are given a genuine dollar bill and told to study it. They spend days learning everything they can about the dollar bill, how it feels in their hands, the texture, the thickness of the paper, and so on, the ultimate goal being how to recognize a fake one. The point being if you know what is real, if you are deeply familiar with the authentic, you can more easily identify what is not. This is an effective illustration of how we may recognize any deception, any lie—however subtle, clever, disguised, or ingenious it may be.

My dad worked in the oil industry most of his life, but his passions were his faith, his family, and working in his wood shop. In the last three years of his life, he was on oxygen twenty-four hours a day and had to have a walker to navigate himself around the house. About the only time he left the house was when he went to church. For the last five months of his life, he was confined to bed, unable to do anything except watch TV and talk on his iPhone (when he could figure out how to use it). It was difficult to watch my superman father tamed by the kryptonite of old age. But, to the very end of that genuine life, my dad remained fixed in his belief, authentic to his core.

There is a level of faith that enables you to transcend the need to fit in. My dad had that kind of faith. It was his greatest gift to me.

"All things are lawful for me," but not all things are helpful. "All things are lawful for me," but I will not be dominated by anything.

1 Corinthians 6:12

It is easy to compartmentalize life. I can be pious with my church friends, rowdy with my drinking friends, professional with my work friends, and successful with my Facebook friends. When I cut through all the masks I wear, I have to decide: Is this who I should be? Is this who I want to be? Is this who I am called to be?

I'm just me when I'm with you
What you see is what is true
Exactly who I am as a person, as a man
I'm just me when I'm with you

Those lines are from a song called "Just Me," a love song I wrote for my wife. Taking a second look at the lyrics, I came to realize how true this could also be concerning the way I am with my Savior. Does he really want me to wear a mask out in the world? I need and want to be the same no matter where I go. By the same token, I know I will always be the most authentic and at ease in the presence of Jesus.

WHO THE CREATURE BELONGS TO

In all the talk about brands and branding, we covered only one aspect of the word: the image we present to the world we live in. But there is another meaning for the word, one we are just as familiar with, and has just as much weight and significance as the one explored above. In the cattle business, as I saw in cowboy films as a kid, the number of cows is pretty impressive. In the bustle, and because of the numbers, to protect the owner of the herd from any confusion of ownership, a simple solution was discovered a long time ago: Take a rod of iron, and affix some design, number, or name to the end of that iron. Heat it to a red-hot glow then press the sizzling end onto the cow's hind parts or thereabouts. It is a *brand*. The rod is called a *branding iron.* This brand means that the animal lawfully belongs to one ranch, one owner, livestock dealer, or whomever. To steal or harm the creature in any way is prohibited. How many westerns that you watched as a kid had cattle rustlers in them?

> Set me as a seal upon your heart, As a seal upon your arm; For love is as strong as death, Jealousy as cruel as the grave; Its flames are flames of fire, A most vehement flame.
>
> **Song of Solomon 8:6, NKJV**

A brand tells the rest of the world who a creature belongs to. (I think you may see where I am going with this, but it is an image that works.) More importantly, it says something definitive about our relationship with Christ. Once you belong to him, you are branded in a sense. Baptism is branding of a kind, or at least an initial part of the process. It uses water instead of hot iron, but the significance is the same. Belonging to Christ is something cultivated in a person, but it begins with a plunge in the fount. It will demand no less than a lifetime of growth and change, of reassessment and repatterning from the deepest parts of us to the surface—from the inside out.

We are continually being shaped into the image of Christ. Why? Because of his great love for us. Because it is his way. It means I now belong to Jesus. It means he has set his seal upon me, upon my heart. "Do not fear," he says, "for I have redeemed you; I have summoned you by name; you are mine" (Isaiah 43:1, NIV). I wear his brand upon my flesh and upon the tablets of my heart. It tells the world who I belong to, that I am most myself when I am his alone.

JUST ME

Jordan Mogey, Buddy Mondlock, Kent Maxson

I wish I had the nerve to say just how I feel
But I sure need this job and it's all part of the deal
So I trade a little soul for insurance and a check
And don't worry about the boot that's on my neck

I've got a satchel full of masks I wear out in the world
There's the one I wear to work and for talking to a girl
There's one for Sunday morning and there's one for the bar
It's easy to lose track of who you are

> Then I see myself reflected in your eyes
> And there I was with no disguise

CHORUS
I'm just me when I'm with you
What you see is what is true
Exactly who I am as a person, as a man
I'm just me when I'm with you

So when I tell the boss, "I think you might be right"
I won't be getting lost, I'm just staying out of sight
I can play the game as well as I need to
If I know I'm going home to you

> Where I can see myself reflected in your eyes
> And there I am with no disguise

No Way Out But Through

CHORUS

I'm just me when I'm with you

What you see is what is true

Exactly who I am as a person, as a man

I'm just me when I'm with you

Chapter 9
A Crisis of Perception

Ever since God created the world his invisible qualities, both his eternal power and his divine nature, have been clearly seen; they are perceived in the things that God has made. So these people have no excuse at all.

Romans 1:20, GNT

For thirty years or so, I worked in the consumer electronics and audio/video industry. I had impressive job titles like "Global Training Manager," most of which required a good bit of travel. My job description for two of the companies required eighty percent travel. I was gone more than half the month—away from my family, the most important people in my life.

In those days, because you were charged by the minute, I carried two cell phones—one for personal calls and one for business. I became a weekend dad. When I called home to speak to my kids, my wife would tell me they were either in bed or doing their homework. My office was in my house, so when a situation arose at work, it would often take me away from my family again. The first thing I did when I got up in the morning and the last thing I did at night was check my work messages. There was a brief time when money got tight, so I held down a second job at our church on the weekends. I did this because I was taking care of my family. Raising four kids is expensive.

I missed a lot of my children's childhood, and I blame no one but myself. The time I lost with my family is time I will never get back. There is nothing wrong with working hard, but at some point, one needs to stop and take inventory, maybe ask a few questions.

How much is enough?

What really matters?

What am I really working for?

The balance of work, family, and God is a delicate one. Without excuse or apology, it is about priorities, about making right choices. The question that supersedes all other questions goes something like this: "In all I do, at home or away from home, do I place God first?" It is not an easy question to ask, any more than it is comfortable to answer. Nor is it one you can easily dissemble, fake, or tiptoe around.

There have been Sundays I slept in because I stayed out too late the night before. Or soccer matches I missed because I had to finish a project for work. Essentially, I made choices based on what was important at that moment, regardless of the priorities God has established. At those moments, I prioritized other things in my life with more regard than I did God or my family. Those choices revealed where my heart was at the time, and to be an inch away is to be miles away.

The line moves all the time, especially today, but I am told that men generally derive their sense of self-worth from their work, whereas women typically find value in relationships. While the normal exercise of either of these conditions, male or female, is no cause for alarm, when taken to extremes neither is healthy or good. God has given us all we need for blessing and fulfillment, both of which are a demonstration of his glory. Paul tells us we have all been given "gifts of the spirit," and that these individual gifts are to be used collectively for the good of God's church (1 Corinthians 12:1, NIV).

So where does perspective come from? How do I escape this entrapment of my time and obligations in this present world and live a life based on the priorities of the world to come? I know, or I strongly suspect, even as I write this, that these questions are common among believers, and that my response and yours, while not easy, become a kind of rite of passage—one of the early hurdles in the life of faith. If you're like me, you have probably done your share of head-scratching over these questions.

But here is another question: *How can an almighty God, himself rather busy with a universe and billions of souls on this lonely little planet, possibly single me out, know every detail of me from the soles of my feet to the very number of hairs on my head, take me under his wing in spite of my brazen humanity, care for and even love me with the articulation, precision, and tender care that he does?* That is a question even a king might ask.

> When I look at your heavens, the work of your fingers, the moon and the stars, which you have set in place, what is man that you are mindful of him, and the son of man that you care for him?
>
> **Psalm 8:3–4**

THE DOORS

As I was writing this chapter, I had to stop. I suddenly became aware that the events in my life, the little corner I had painted myself into, were crowding out the joy. I was losing perspective—or had lost so much of it.

No Way Out But Through

When perception becomes cloudy, everything is askew. I didn't think to call it this at the time, but I was having a crisis of perception.

One of the musical groups I was weaned on as a kid was The Doors. Their lead singer and large personality was a guy named Jim Morrison. Details about Morrison or the band are not important here, but I remember hearing that the group got its name from a quote by eighteenth and early nineteenth-century English poet and artist William Blake. I did a little digging and discovered that it was taken from a book called *The Marriage of Heaven and Hell* (1790). I haven't read the disturbingly titled little book and can't tell if the passage even fits in a Christian context. Nor am I sure it matters, but it adds a bit of clarity to this discussion.

> If the doors of perception were cleansed, everything would appear to man as it is, Infinite.
>
> **William Blake (1757–1827),**
> *The Marriage of Heaven and Hell*

This is the whole issue—of my personal quest for righteousness, freedom, and clarity and yours. It is the entire point of this chapter, if not the entire book that once our perception is cleansed, we will begin to see with a new clarity. New paths will be illumined before us, ones we will recognize as just and right and with the print of sandaled feet before us. We will hear new things from those around us, discover new depths—not only in ourselves but also in others. The words of God will suddenly be alive in ways not possible before.

With these things in mind, I took a couple of hours and drove to a secluded place to take a walk around a small lake. Somehow, I had to drown out the roar of the city; I had to be alone with God. Although God is everywhere, his presence has a way of becoming more distinct when I am alone with him in nature, however sophisticated or not that isolation may be. When I walk through the woods, I pray—nothing grand or wordy, just the immediacy of my heart, tiny thoughts finding a voice. They drift on the air then are gone to do their strange work. The more I give my thoughts and feelings the freedom to soar, the more I feel the presence of God. He misses nothing—or I am convinced he misses nothing. That, too, is a consequence of perception.

According to the *Oxford English Dictionary*, to perceive is "to apprehend with the mind; to become aware or conscious of; to realize; to discern, observe. To interpret or look on (a thing, situation, person, etc.) in a particular way." If those doors of perception are opaque, blurred, or contaminated with noise, perception cannot help but suffer and mislead. The Bible defines the process, that step toward clarity, and in a way that it has little choice but to sing.

> One thing I do know. I was blind but now I see!
>
> **John 9:25, NIV**

I live in Nashville, Tennessee. Millions of people come here every year to enjoy the clubs, the bars, the historical sites, and, most importantly, the music. We live about a mile from Broadway, the city's main entertainment district. The amount of humanity that can be crammed into this small area of town is immense, and it's always moving. When you live in a big city like Nashville, it is easy for your senses to become overwhelmed. It is impossible to see the stars at night because of the streetlights and the ambient light illuminating the night sky. Day and night, you can hear the low drone of the interstate traffic mixed with the sounds of sirens in the distance—the music and the party atmosphere on the streets.

No Way Out But Through

To try and protect our sanity, my wife and I decided to invest in a tiny home on top of a mountain about an hour-and-a-half drive away from Nashville. That little four-hundred-square-foot building has become our getaway sanctuary. Nestled in the woods, it is far enough away from anything resembling civilization, that we go for midnight walks and gaze at the stars, listening to the wind blowing through the trees, the trilling of crickets. During the day, we hike on trails by a creek that leads to a hidden waterfall. In the mornings, we sit on the deck and drink our coffee, the music of creation all around us. With the coolness of morning on my face, I am surrounded by a calm that transcends the moment, a peace I experience nowhere else. Our tiny home is situated in a place resembling Eden.

In the first few passages of the Bible, we are given the order of creation. God's first recorded act was to speak light into darkness, to bring order to chaos. Once he did this, he could perform the work he set out to do. His first utterance was "Light be!" And there was light. He saw it, and he saw that the light was good. It was very good. With that note, we have the first day, then the next, then the next, and so on. Six days of making stuff, and one more to rest and take it all in. It was a good week.

First there was chaos. Then there was light. With the light came order and the fullness of creation. It is the same with you and me. When the light of perception comes—and all the visibility, clarity, awareness, and sparkle that come with it—then comes order, clearing a way for wisdom and creative thinking. Made in his image, it is written in our DNA, or deeper. We are co-creators with God, particularly in the life he has given us. The good, hard, and excellent work of cleansing my "doors of perception," is not up to me alone. I cannot cleanse or save myself. But I can do my part. As mentioned earlier, this is a cooperative work between me and God. I do 100 percent and God does 100 percent. It is an extraordinary math, but it works. Some things are going to remain a mystery; there was a reason he warned against eating from the Tree of the Knowledge of Good and Evil. The point is cooperation between me and God. Like salvation, like forgiveness, love, faith, and other things, it is a daily, ongoing work.

THIS SIDE OF HEAVEN

We have been enjoying the resources of God's creation for a very long time. And it is only right. It was made for you and me. According to the Bible, the earth and its resources are ours to subdue, to work, to feed upon, and to enjoy. And though the end will come, there remains a grandness we may still behold, a beauty and mystery—the stars, the planets, the unfathomable beyond, the sky at dusk or at dawn, the roll of the ocean, the mystery of its depths, the flight of an eagle, things beyond our imagining—that leave us quiet, without speech, things best remembered and clarified by a poet.

> There are three things that are too amazing for me, four that I do not understand: the way of an eagle in the sky, the way of a snake on a rock, the way of a ship on the high seas, and the way of a man with a young maiden.
>
> **Proverbs 30:18–19, NIV**

When I look into the night sky, I like to think I am looking at a canvas that was painted by God, an image of infinity itself (as I am able to understand it). So, what is it about looking into infinity that inspires? The Bible says, "The skies proclaim the work of his hands" (Psalm 19:1, NIV). What he has made transcends time. When we experience his handiwork, we are living and moving and having our being, so to speak, as a part of an even greater canvas. You and I are a part of that creation, part of his handiwork, remembering that on day six, he created man in his own image.

We were created without sin, for sin had no dominion yet in the world. The particulars on how sin entered the world, how it set up shop or found its way in the consciousness of man, is a story for another book, but through nature we are allowed a glimpse of what freedom from sin is like. So many times as we wander through life, we reach out to God, wanting to hear from him. While we beg to hear his voice, we forget or little think of the multitude of ways in which he does communicate with us. He has made many forms of communication and detection by which we can hear, see, and feel him. Sadly, many of us in our well-meaning passion to hear, feel, or see God have counterfeited those very sensations. In that sense, we rush ahead of him. In doing so, in our attempts to "conjure" him with soft music, chants, endless prayers, and so on—as worthy as those things are, as effective as they are at times—we do not allow God to be God. He will speak to us in any fashion he pleases, ways that cannot be predicted or managed. It is his game. He created the chess board, all the pieces, and all that play on it. That is a crude image perhaps, but you get the point. He *alone* is God, in spite of our attempts to usurp his power, in spite of our technologies and our universities that suggest so vehemently otherwise. He speaks to us through his Word and through other believers, but he can and does communicate to us as well (and as thoroughly) through his creation, which is as perennial as the ocean and the pageantry of stars in the heavens.

There is a yearning I suspect we all feel, a deep gulf within each of us, a hollow place only God can possibly fill. It became a part of human existence as soon as he breathed life into Adam, and perhaps it became even more pronounced once Adam was forced to leave Eden. In spite of this, God has provided infinite ways to fellowship with him, some we may not have thought of. We can enjoy communion with him through his creation, in the subtleties of his movement in and through us, as he touches our senses with revelation and by a clarity that changes everything. We have no need to "conjure" him. We do not need to activate the usual props anymore. He is supreme over them, and he is in the business of reaching us. Man may have been tossed out of Eden, he may have walked out all gloomy and hush, scratching his head in the whirlwind of a what-was-that kind of moment, but that doesn't mean that the garden was closed down for business. Paradise has a reach of its own. It is a mystical place, but it is still present. Where? In love, in the exercise of the gospel, in the next act of kindness. A syllogism can help: God is love. Paradise is where God communes with man. Love, therefore, is paradise present. It is in us, in you and me, where we allow it access, in community where it can flourish.

My father had a wood shop full of every wood-crafting tool known to man. Through the years, he honed his carpentry skills and learned to make exquisite pieces of furniture. My mother is a seamstress who can sew and create almost any piece of clothing you could want. Along the way, she started making quilts and has won multiple awards for the quilts she made. My older sister, Debbie, followed in my mother's footsteps and sews clothes for children. My sister Joan decorates intricately designed cakes. Creativity was a natural part of my household. Now, I see it in my children. I write songs—I hack away at it every day as another random thought or some movement in me becomes a song. I am blessed that way. But creativity, far from being the domain or inheritance of the precious few, is available to all of us. To be created in the image of God is to be like him. We can be co-creators with him. We have been given the proper tools, written like a song deep into the confines of our DNA, and, whether we realize it or not, we engage this part of us all the time in ways both small and large. It may not be in the aesthetic sense, like the poet, the singer-songwriter, or another Leonardo, but in every decision we make there is an element of the creative, of the God part of us.

There is no job or task in the world that has not been improved through the creative process, that has not been touched by its joy and freedom. Exploring possibilities while you follow certain known rules of construction leads you down multiple paths as you pursue the completion of a project. But once the task is done, there is a moment when you look at the final results and relish both the journey and its conclusion. There is such a sense of joy and accomplishment when you successfully create something independently. Remember: At the end of every day, even God "saw that it was good." There also exists, if but in a flash, a sense of "How did I do that?" It is an honest question born out of the truth that you do 100 percent of the work while God does his 100 percent. The fact that God is a part of the mechanism is also a good check of our humility. Humility notwithstanding, there is something special about the moment when you take a step back and admire a finished work. This is exactly what God did after completing the creation of the world.

> And God saw everything that he had made, and behold, it was
> very good.
> **Genesis 1:31**

A hard day's work is nature's answer for insomnia. The best sleep I ever experienced was at the end of a long, excruciating day of purposeful work. When your work has purpose, it magnifies contentment, and your rest has validity. When you are spent, when exhaustion comes from labor for the kingdom, life has meaning. The second your head hits the pillow, the ache in your body and mind fades into a deep and restful sleep full of contentment, fulfillment, and sweet dreams.

God, family, work—it seems pretty simple. Clearing away the debris from our perception allows us to better prioritize life. The result is balance, equilibrium. Taking time for solitude and meditation helps, being alone with your own thoughts and allowing God access. It will take a bit of discipline, but any exercise of value will ask the same. Look up. See what God has done. Once you are surrounded by his artwork, if you are paying attention, you will sense his presence. You will start to become familiar with it and with its character. In time, you will come to recognize and avoid its counterfeits. You will come to know what is really important—what to pursue and what not to. You will know what you are called to do, and, even better, you will know yourself in a new and delightful way.

MINNOW

Kent Maxson, Randy Finchum

Had enough of the bright lights, the sirens and the traffic

So I put my two weeks in, climbed down the corporate ladder,

Sold our downtown condo, bought a little piece of land

Traded headaches and high blood pressure for these blisters on my
hands

> **CHORUS**
>
> Now it's coffee on the front porch
>
> Wind chimes dancing in the breeze
>
> Waving at my neighbors
>
> While they're waving back at me
>
> Was a big fish in the ocean and a gator in the swamp
>
> Now I'm just a minnow, but I sure love my pond

We're laying on a blanket in the back of a flatbed Ford

Miles from the city on a moonlit country road

Stars in the heavens sprinkled across the sky like sand

Got a front row seat to a masterpiece painted by the good Lord's
hand

> **CHORUS**
>
> Now it's coffee on the front porch
>
> Wind chimes dancing in the breeze
>
> Waving at my neighbors
>
> While they're waving back at me

No Way Out But Through

Was a big fish in the ocean and a gator in the swamp

Now I'm just a minnow, but I sure love my pond

BRIDGE

Sun peeks over the water at the break of dawn

We both fell asleep stayed here all night long

Chapter 10
And Who Is My Neighbor?

Adam blamed Eve, Eve blamed the snake
But we're the ones responsible for the choices that we make

Kent Maxson and Randy Finchum, "Cindy and Jamie"

One night, my wife and I went to dinner at a restaurant near our home. There was a new waitress there whom I will call Robin. Robin was very friendly and an exceptional waitress. Cindy and I thought she was charming, and we enjoyed a lot of light conversation with her. At one point she mentioned that her boyfriend was trying to get into music. I like to meet and help young songwriters, so I gave her my business card and told her to have her boyfriend contact me if he ever wanted to write a song or record something in my studio. A couple of years later, at around ten o'clock in the evening, my cell phone rang with a number I didn't recognize. Thinking it was an unwanted sales call, I let it go to voicemail. A few minutes later I noticed a message, so I checked, and it was from Robin. At first, I couldn't remember who she was, but Cindy reminded me, so I finished listening to her voicemail. It sounded like she might be in distress, so I immediately returned her call. She told me who she was and how we had met and that she had kept my card for the last couple of years just in case she needed it. She then told me she needed help. She had no gas in her car and had been evicted from her apartment because she had lost her job and couldn't pay the rent. Everything she owned was in her car, and all she wanted was some gas money, a little food and a place to stay for the night. My wife and I talked it over and decided to meet her at the convenience store where she said she had run out of gas.

When we got to her, she was very disoriented. We couldn't decide if she was so traumatized that she was shaking or if she was maybe going through withdrawal from something. She assured us she was not using drugs, but that she had a prescription for antianxiety medication she could not afford to refill. She said her cell phone was going to be cut off the next day because she had not paid her bill for a couple of months. For all our good intentions, my wife and I did not know what to do. We didn't know if Robin was trying to scam us or if we should believe her story and try to help her somehow. We chose to help her and see where it would lead.

We told Robin we would help her but if we found any evidence of her using drugs, she would be on her own. We filled her gas tank. We bought her a disposable phone with some prepaid minutes. We then took her to our house to shower and clean up. We gave her a good home-cooked meal, complete with my wife's homemade wheat bread, and told her she could stay the night.

We use the second floor of our home as an Airbnb. It is a very large space with three bedroom suites and a sleeping loft that will comfortably sleep twelve to fourteen people. It was close to Christmas, and we had no one booked, so we gave Robin one of the bedroom suites upstairs. While

Robin took a hot shower, Cindy washed her clothes; they looked and smelled like they had not been washed in weeks.

Robin slept until a little past noon, and when she came downstairs to join us, we could see she was still very agitated and distraught. In the course of our conversation that morning she told us multiple times that she had thoughts of harming herself, that she was suicidal. Cindy and I decided we needed to talk to Robin about going to Vanderbilt hospital for psychological evaluation. We approached her cautiously with this proposal and she slowly warmed to the idea. We took her to the hospital and helped her get settled in. Since we were not related to Robin, we were kept in the dark about her condition. We still didn't know if she was truly suicidal or simply strung out on drugs. We were told she would be there for a couple of weeks.

Over the next two weeks, one of us visited Robin every day. We asked her questions about her family and friends and made the usual small talk— nothing to upset her. We learned about her troubled childhood and how she ended up in Nashville. On some visits she was agitated and distraught, like the night she first called us. On other occasions she was warm and charming, like the evening we first met her as our waitress. Cindy and I went back and forth about what we should do when Robin got out of the hospital.

Robin was released from the hospital about a week before Christmas, and we decided we would let her stay with us until she could get a job. On Christmas Day we invited her to join us as we celebrated with our family. My wife and I have eleven children between us, so our Christmas celebration can get crowded. Not everyone made it that particular year, but we still had a large gathering. We put a couple presents for Robin under the tree and included her in our meal and family time.

Over the next few weeks, we watched Robin come and go, and we listened as she told us about the job interviews she had been to. Each trip was followed by a hard-luck story of why she didn't get the job and why she needed more money. On a couple of these occasions, we loaned her some money to help her with bills she said she needed to pay. But we became more aware of the odd hours she was keeping, and stories about her job interviews and the places she had to go got more strange and unusual. The longer she stayed, the more uneasy and suspicious we became.

One morning, Robin hurried out of the house to meet someone who was going to help her get a job as a caregiver. Not long after she left, we heard a phone ring. Robin had left the burner phone we had given her on the table. Then a text message popped up on the screen; part of it was an inquiry about sexual favors in exchange for drugs. Robin was buying, selling, and using drugs while using our home as a safehouse.

If shock was my first reaction, rage was a close second. Forced to come to terms with an awful situation, I asked myself, "How could she do this to us? How could anybody do this to my wife and me? How could we have been so foolish?"

The girl we tried to help used us. We decided not to let her stay any longer, but we also felt that to communicate that in anger was wrong. We felt we had to show love in spite of how we had been played. My stepson and I went upstairs and packed all of Robin's clothes and belongings into some large black trash bags and placed them downstairs by the front door. Throwing together all the clothes and Christmas gifts we had given her just a few weeks earlier brought up some conflicting emotions. We then watched from the front window for her car. My heart started racing as she parked at the curb and started to walk up the sidewalk toward our front door. As Cindy opened the door, my stepson and I picked up the bags full of Robin's possessions and took them to her car.

Cindy stopped Robin at the door and told her she would not be staying here anymore. She then calmly told Robin how we knew that she had lied and manipulated us. At this point, Robin, with a performance we could only consider well-rehearsed, tried to convince us of her innocence and how she had been persecuted. Cindy held her ground and restated the facts as we had discovered them. She wished Robin good luck, told her we would pray for her, and closed the door.

It would be easy for me or anyone in my position to throw stones at Robin, metaphorically or otherwise. I have never taken illegal drugs. I have my own share of sins that I have wrestled with and attempted to hide from the world. But Robin's story allows me to make a point without having to expose my own crimes, even though I can read the scroll of those crimes as they pass like endless movie credits through my awareness. My thought was to relate some incident, some crime against God that I could share with Robin which would make a point yet not make me look too bad. As the credits scrolled, I weighed each of them, wondering which one(s) I might frame into a narrative that did me minimal damage. Do I talk about the time I had a little too much to drink? Do I go tell the secrets of my darkest, most hidden, and repulsive sins? I was hoping to make a point about being a Christian without tarnishing the shining armor of my faith.

It was easy to compare my sins with hers, especially because hers were so raw, so new, and fresh—imagining I could claim some sainthood in the comparison. But that's just not the truth. It may be true that we have all done things that we are too ashamed to utter even to ourselves at times— even those crimes, as mine feel to be, that violate everything I profess to believe. In this one chapter, I have written paragraph after paragraph of detail on the crimes against my wife and me, those committed by a lost young girl, dedicating only a single paragraph, maybe a second, to declare my own.

Do you see my dilemma?

Maybe you detect already how this entire debacle, if I let it, might grant me the courage and good judgment to face my own crimes. Hers are no better or worse in the bigger picture. It might let me see, if I allow myself, whether I believe anything I say I believe—whether I have any understanding of how justice and mercy work, how I cannot be harmed no matter how many Robins I encounter, or whatever she or anyone else may take from me. She cannot harm me.

Let me put it in a more biblical way: Dead men and women cannot be harmed. How is that for a response? When we come to Christ, that is part of the dynamic. To be like Christ, to know him, is to know and become like him in his death. It is, indeed, a martyrdom of a kind. There may be a better word for it, but martyrdom works for now.

I am, or I want to be, a man after God's own heart. To be "after" God, is to be in continuous pursuit of him, to do as he asks—that is, to hug the cactus, as Mel Gibson says (face your own truths, dark as they may be). If you will be his disciples (God's, not Gibson's), if you will follow him, you will know the pain of your own sin. It is the pain of death, but once you embrace that particular death, you take your first step toward freedom and no harm can possibly come to you. All the Robins in the world suddenly come into right perspective. Our eyes are cleansed. We can see the infinite, even for a broken creature like Robin. If God is to have and enjoy any glory from this situation with her, I have no choice. I must deny myself. I must deny my wife, in a sense, or any feeling or impulse of revenge or punishment that Robin inspired in me.

We are all familiar with the story of the woman who was caught in the act of adultery by the Pharisees. We know adultery is wrong. I mean, it may have less gravity in our culture today, but it is nonetheless a biblical mandate. Either way, the Pharisees were serious. Before double-minded, hypocritical, mean-spirited zealots, a woman like that becomes an easy target for their twisted judgment. With rocks in their hands and that weird justice aflame in their religious hearts, they pressed Jesus to condemn the woman.

Fools. Knowing their duplicity, Jesus, very coolly, bends down and writes something with his finger in the dirt. What he said next blew out their fire and made the very rocks, which at other times may cry out, go mute in their hands, even as the words in their mouths. With the best comeback ever recorded, Jesus said:

> Let him who is without sin among you be the first to throw a
> stone at her.
>
> **John 8:7**

If you're like me, you have read multiple commentaries about what Jesus was writing in the sand. Some of them may preach well, but many of them are a real stretch, pound the pulpit as we might. One author suggests that Jesus was writing out the sins of those in the crowd. Another said he was writing down their names. Another said Scripture. Another said he was doodling, biding his time until the fury of the moment reached such a pitch that he could intervene and not just save the woman's life but give the rock-throwers a chance to change their ways. True or not, the point is we judge quickly when, in truth, judgment is not ours.

The law of Jesus doesn't behave according to the old Mosaic fashion. His mercy is as deep and as wide and as full as the sea. Who could understand such a thing? My guess is that the angry crowd could not get it, but the woman did. That scene makes her the main character. "Go, and. . . sin no more," was all Jesus had to say to her (John 8:11). In that moment, she was poised to listen unlike at any other time in her life. Though we beat this passage to death with commentary, opinion after opinion, the wisdom of Jesus is always to the point, always easy to understand, and always touches the heart in all the right places, as precise as heaven itself—always on time, always trustworthy.

Why do you see the speck that is in your brother's eye, but do not notice the log that is in your own eye?

Luke 6:41

WHAT WERE WE THINKING?

It is generally not a good idea to write a song about two prostitutes strung out on cocaine, then give one of them your wife's name and the other your cowriter's wife's name. But that is exactly what Randy Finchum and I did. With lines like "Jamie was a cheerleader, and Cindy the prom queen / Till the needle and the crack pipe took away their dreams," we may have shot ourselves in the foot, as the saying goes, or sabotaged our own wellbeing. (I am still trying to explain it all to Cindy.) In spite of a real miscalculation on our parts, there is something to learn from this little cautionary tale. One, don't ever use your wife's name in a song about prostitutes and drug addicts unless you want to sleep outside with the dog. Two, there is no Two. Just memorize rule number one.

All that aside, it is much easier to create a narrative about someone else's shortcomings, even if you have never experienced the things they have or know any of the particulars they have dealt with. I have been around cocaine. I have seen the behavior, effect, and aftereffects, if only on some TV crime show, the same crime shows that depict hookers and addicts. In a three-minute song there is not a lot of room for detail. To turn that scrutiny in on oneself is another story; I would rather the narrative of my own life, my own crimes and miscalculations of judgment, remain hidden. That is why many turn to religion. Religion is about blind obedience to a set of made-up principles, some of them good, most of them irrelevant. Either way, it provides a convenient place to hide. Anyone can come to church on time, sing a song, pray, and even cry on cue. But loving someone sacrificially? Helping the prostitute or addict instead of judging them? Loving your neighbor as yourself? Saying what needs to be said regardless of how uncomfortable? Those things represent the hard work of the gospel. The men holding rocks in their hands were very religious.

What we are after is grown-up perspective, to live out a grown-up gospel. Religion is an excuse for having neither. Anyone can do religion. But few can carry that cross daily and give of themselves fully without expectation of anything in return.

> *Jesus sees a princess and the pimp just sees a whore*
> *Preacher sees them through the windshield, looks ahead and locks the*
>   *door*
> *I wish that I could see this old world through different eyes*
> *I know what others should do, but when it comes to me I'm blind*
> *Adam blamed Eve, Eve blamed the snake*
> *But we're the ones responsible for the choices that we make*

This is one of the most complex songs I have ever attempted to write (or explain). It is all about having different eyes, which is something you can't give yourself no matter how many times you go to church, raise your hands, or sing another worship song. Do I pass judgment on others while I drive by and do nothing to help? Do I minimize and then blame others for my sins while passing judgment on them? Who's to blame for each sin? What are we responsible for? Where is grace in all this? Once, a man came to Jesus and asked him, "Who is my neighbor?" Here is how Jesus responded to the man:

> "A man was going down from Jerusalem to Jericho, and he fell among robbers, who stripped him and beat him and departed, leaving him half dead. Now by chance a priest was going down

that road, and when he saw him he passed by on the other side. So likewise a Levite, when he came to the place and saw him, passed by on the other side. But a Samaritan, as he journeyed, came to where he was, and when he saw him, he had compassion. He went to him and bound up his wounds, pouring on oil and wine. Then he set him on his own animal and brought him to an inn and took care of him. And the next day he took out two denarii and gave them to the innkeeper, saying, 'Take care of him, and whatever more you spend, I will repay you when I come back.' Which of these three, do you think, proved to be a neighbor to the man who fell among the robbers?" He said, "The one who showed him mercy." And Jesus said to him, "You go, and do likewise."

Luke 10:29–37

I shared "Cindy and Jamie" with my friend Kent Blazy, one of my songwriting heroes and mentors. Kent told me that it was a well-written song, but no one would ever listen to it or buy it because it was too uncomfortably real. I took that as a backhanded compliment. I believe he was correct: No one really wants to face the reality of our fallen world. We don't want to be reminded in song of what we have to live through every day. But how can we be a good Samaritan if we cannot confront our own sinfulness? How can we ever hope to show kindness and make a difference in this world if we put blinders on and walk on the other side of the road?

So I unapologetically share this song with you hoping that you will not ignore it or turn it off because it is depressing, unsettling, or simply too real. I challenge you to do what I struggle to do: face and deal with the complexities of this world (including those complexities inside you) and of your faith. Challenge every thought you have and lift up unending prayers to God—always asking for wisdom, guidance, and the strength to discern and do his will. My wife will forgive me. Because she loves me, I am forgiven. That is what love does. That is what it always does.

CINDY & JAMIE

Randy Finchum, Kent Maxson

Cindy's from Oklahoma, Jamie's from Arkansas
Working the street corner on the north side of Omaha
Jamie was a cheerleader and Cindy the prom queen
Till the needle and the crack pipe took away their dreams

CHORUS

Jesus sees a princess and the pimp just sees a whore
Preacher sees them through the windshield, looks ahead and
locks the door
I wish that I could see this old world through different eyes
I know what others should do, but when it comes to me I'm
blind
Adam blamed Eve, Eve blamed the snake
But we're the ones responsible for the choices that we make

Daddy remembers the day his little girl was born
Innocent in diapers crawling across the floor
The devil stole his angel, what did he do wrong?
He's on his knees every night, praying she'll come home

CHORUS

Jesus sees a princess and the pimp just sees a whore
Preacher sees them through the windshield, looks ahead and
locks the door
I wish that I could see this old world through different eyes

I know what others should do, but when it comes to me I'm
  blind
Adam blamed Eve, Eve blamed the snake
But we're the ones responsible for the choices that we make

She can sleep on the streets or with her landlord
The drugs she needs to numb the pain only cause her more
A twenty buys her body but it sure kills the soul
Such a high price to pay just to get the dope

Chapter 11
Miracles: An Alteration in Nature

As we look not to the things that are seen but to the things that are unseen. For the things that are seen are transient, but the things that are unseen are eternal.

2 Corinthians 4:18

My biggest accomplishment to date as a songwriter is "From Where I'm Sitting," a song I wrote with Garth Brooks. Gary Allan recorded it and placed it on his first album *Used Heart for Sale*. Allan released it as a single in 1997. This album sold enough copies to be certified as a gold record by the Recording Industry Association of America. Having a song on that album opened many doors to me in the music industry. It marked the accomplishment of one of my lifelong dreams and changed my life in countless ways—ways that could fill books, not just a chapter.

So how did I get to write with Garth Brooks?

I was introduced to Garth by his manager Bob Doyle, who thought we might be a good fit as co-writers. I met Bob through a representative at

ASCAP who gave me Bob's new phone number after he'd quit ASCAP to become the manager of a new artist he was going to manage (Garth). I was talking to the representative at ASCAP because Randall "Tex" Cobb and his wife, Sharon (also a songwriter), had listened to some of my songs and told me to call ASCAP and ask for Bob. I'd met Randall and Sharon when I was a salesman at Circuit City. When I sold them a new stereo, I agreed to put it together for them if they would listen to my songs and maybe offer me some guidance. I had been at Circuit City because a friend at church told me about an ad in the paper that said the store was hiring. I happened to be at that church because some friends, Earnie and Katherine Hyne, let me stay at their house for three days when I first moved to Nashville. I had met them through another friend, Mark, who was their son-in-law. I knew Mark from my church group in Lubbock. I had attended that church because my girlfriend went there. Writing this reminds me just how delicate and yet how certain the links are that brought me to Nashville and led to my meeting and writing with Garth Brooks.

Bear with me for a few more details.

While still in Texas, a couple of months after my girlfriend and I broke up, I'd called her to see if there was a chance that we would get back together. Her no was swift and emphatic. "Why don't you just move to Nashville to pursue your music? It's what you've always wanted to do." I was shocked because I didn't remember ever saying that I wanted to move to Nashville. I'd always thought my music would fit best in Los Angeles. Not long after, I shared that story with Mark while at a church function. He said he would ask if I could stay with his in-laws in Nashville.

Before leaving Lubbock, I had to tie up some loose ends. Being part of a music group at the time, I promised them I would stay and finish the album we were working on and play the few last shows that were already on our calendar. On September 18, 1983, the night before I was to leave for Nashville,

I was on stage singing when my ex-girlfriend walked in with another friend of mine. She made her way to the front table by the stage and sat in his lap while we completed the show. Talk about adding insult to injury. The wound still raw, it was tough seeing her all over this guy, old salt-in-the-wound herself, my old love. I remember thinking, "I'm standing up here dying, and you're sitting down there acting like a fool."

Over the next five years I repeated that line over and over, haunted by the thing and the image associated with it, trying new combinations and twists to flesh out what possibilities it might have. It had country song written all over it—the lost love, the ache, the lonesome howl in a man's soul. It was a powerful moment in my life, and it had too strong of a presence in my head to let it go. I was certain I would be able to use it in a song or something. Stuck in my head as it was, it finally came to me how to put my experience that night in Lubbock into words, maybe even find some freedom from it through my art. In my second writing session with Garth, I presented the title "From Where I'm Sitting."

Garth and I wrote this song in 1988. I left Nashville and returned to Texas in December 1991, thinking I would never write another song and would never return to Nashville. Through the years, multiple artists recorded and performed "From Where I'm Sitting," but when it came time to choose songs for their albums, it never made the cut. Then Gary Allan came along.

If you have followed this little history, you may be wondering, what's the point? The point is that we miss miracles because we expect them to be a single unexplained event, when many times they are a series of little steps—some of them large and telling, but most of them quiet and incidental, at least by appearance. One of the biggest "miracles" of my life was a gold record I earned as a songwriter. Life was just carrying on as usual. The links I listed above were just the events, again, both small and large, hidden or otherwise, that took place from 1982 to 1997. The miracle unwound over years, hidden from the eyes of most people.

God works most often in ways beyond what we are capable of detecting. Truth is, his work is displayed all around us, and he reveals what he reveals when he chooses to reveal it. His business is his business. If *I will be what I will be* is his name, *I will do what I will do the way I choose to do it* is hidden in that name. Even so, as the Scripture says, the heavens actually do declare the glory of God, the sky his handiwork, the seas, the earth, and so on. He has made himself very plain, and if we had the necessary forensic skills or the ability to look back into time, his actions are not as hidden as we might think. Indeed, they are displayed everywhere, from the family album to that conversation you had with a stranger at Starbucks. You get the picture. C. S. Lewis said it in his usual C. S. Lewis way:

> Miracles are a retelling in small letters of the very same story which is written across the whole world in letters too large for some of us to see.
>
> **C. S. Lewis,** *Miracles*

His point and mine is that though we cannot see it, the miracle is there in plain sight. There are times he will let us in on his business, and plainly too. Even so, it has been my experience that the chess God plays has such phenomenal reach, his moves so remote and untranslatable, so far from our ability to detect one move or the other, that to us it becomes a miracle only at its manifestation or emergence. To him, it's just his daily routine— each step being its own small miracle until the larger one arrives. And don't think it ends, or the music stops once the water becomes wine. That is just another step. Miracles are living, thriving, ever-evolving things. If he knows the number of hairs on our heads, as Scripture assures us he does, he knows the end from the beginning.

According to Webster's, a miracle is "an effect or extraordinary event in the physical world that surpasses all known human or natural powers and is ascribed to a supernatural cause. Such an effect or event manifesting or considered as a work of God." That is fine, but what Webster's doesn't say is that for those who believe, miracles can become commonplace.

We are told that the first miracle performed by Jesus was turning water into wine. It took place at a wedding at Cana of Galilee. His mother was there. At first glance, it may seem like an event that took place in an instant, unrelated to anything that came before, a mere response to his mother's bidding. And we are all familiar with the condensed version of the narrative. Mom says, "We're out of wine. Do something, son!" Son says, "Woman, why do you bother me? My time has not yet come." In spite of what appears like aggravation, he does as his mother asks.

> Jesus said to the servants, "Fill the jars with water." And they
> filled them up to the brim. And he said to them, "Now draw
> some out and take it to the master of the feast." So they took it.
>
> John 2:7–8

And *voila*! We have wine. Water goes into the jug. Wine comes out. The servants scratch their heads, look at each other with surprise, but carry on. It's their job. It's also a bona fide miracle. There were no hidden pipes, no tricks of perception or sleight of hand. It was a legitimate and deliberate act of divinity. Not only that, it marked the beginning of Jesus's ministry, his "coming out" party, so to speak. His debut.

Thank God for mothers.

Forgive my levity, but it is easy to believe in miracles when something spectacular happens in an instant—something that baffles us and leaves us scratching our own heads, those unforgettable, unrepeatable moments that reach outside and beyond nature, turning something that *is not* into something that *is*, some alteration in nature, plucking the natural from the *super*-natural. But a miracle has a foreground that neither you nor I are able to discern, stitched together by many seemingly unrelated parts and steps over a long stretch of time and distance.

And don't miss the fact that this first miracle of Jesus came as a result of obedience—Jesus being obedient to his mother's request and the servants being obedient to Jesus's commands. There is a direct and powerful relationship between obedience and the miraculous.

MILES AND MILES OF TIME

Who other than God is able to say when or where a miracle starts? All the links mentioned above were part of the long chain of events that led to what I consider a major miracle in my life. I vividly remember praying to God as early as my fourth-grade year in school when I was eight years old that my music would be "heard around the world." It is an old prayer, but the links were in motion even then, and even before then, before I thought to pray. Was that eight-year-old's prayer random and self-inspired, or was it, like the servants', an act of obedience? Did I pray on my own, or was I prompted by some power outside myself? How far had that prayer whistled and scurried through time to get to me? Boom! This means from before the time I started praying to God for this to happen until it officially happened was a time span of at least thirty-two years. Or was it more years than I can count?

Our minds do not process these things easily. It takes an exercise, perhaps a continuous exercise, of faith to understand them. We see a miracle as an instantaneous event, some spontaneous alteration of nature. But did God ignore my prayers for thirty-one years, then one day decide to answer them because my faith had changed for the better, because I had been a good boy? Or, during those same thirty-one years, did he put into motion countless tiny events and bring them to fruition at a specific moment in time, a moment of his own choosing? The latter is more likely.

And did my prayer initiate anything, or was it simply part of a continuum of prayers that resulted in something wonderful, only for that "something wonderful" to have life beyond itself into the unknown of my own future, of one of my offspring, or of some passerby who happened to hear my song on the radio? It happens.

My friend, David Teems, has two recordings where he speaks Scripture over ambient music. One is called *Hope*, the other *More Hope*. He told me the story of how they came to be, and I want to share the condensed version. Years ago, David was in full-time music ministry. An itinerant minister, David sang and spoke in churches all over the country. One day, a young girl of nineteen came to David and his wife, Benita, in serious need of help. She was suicidal. She had been to Christian counselors, but nothing seemed to help. It was at that time, that Janie (fictitious name) came to David and Benita at their office in Atlanta. After listening to Janie's story, David said he had no idea what to do. He had a bachelor's degree in psychology, but so what? He had no credentials for that kind of therapy. But it wasn't therapy she needed.

Having sung in so many different kinds of churches—Assembly of God one week, Southern Baptist the next, Roman Catholic the week after that, Episcopal and Church of God the weeks and months after that—David had been gravitating toward Scripture since Scripture seemed to be the only thing any of these churches had in common or could agree on. Thinking of Janie and how divided her soul was, he thought about giving Scripture a try.

It worked.

He recorded Scripture for Janie. But not just any Scripture, not even the "power" Scriptures most of us turn to under threat. He chose Scripture that dealt with pain and heartache—from Job, Psalms, Isaiah, Jeremiah, the words of Jesus and Paul, Scripture with exceptional poetic weight and charm. The powerful lyricism and movement of poetry, he felt, might be able to penetrate in ways regular prose may not, however well-written. He kept this recording to one theme: the love of God. There was no huge block of Scripture from any one place in the Bible, but he wove passages together seamlessly in a logical procession—again, according to the music in the lines. He put ambient sounds behind the voiceover, whatever he had available—ocean sounds, Gregorian chant, soft solo piano, and so on. He recorded a crude thirty-minute cassette and gave it to Janie and asked her to listen to it as much as she could. And she did. She listened to this recording over and over, passed it around to other girls in the home where she was living, and listened again.

In time, Janie came out of her depression, got a job, and gradually became a responsible member of society. There was now stability where before her footing was perilously unsure. David will say that just the act of kindness may have been enough, but I think it was more than that. It was the power of the Word itself that penetrated a young girl's troubled heart and made it whole again. The best of miracles.

But the story doesn't end there. One miracle often finds a way to turn into another.

After that strange and glorious event, David scripted and recorded two CDs worth of the same type of Scripture and ambient music with themes like hunger, the love of God, loneliness, thirst, joy, etc. One is called *Hope*, the other is *More Hope*. A couple of years later, one of the selections from *More Hope* called "I Chose You" was picked as that year's top selection on a Billy Graham radio station in Black Mountain, North Carolina. Many of the Scriptures on Janie's recording were on "I Chose You." Around that same time, late one evening, a radio host at a Greenville, South Carolina, station felt she should play "I Chose You." A man happened to be driving on a mountain road that night, who, like Janie, wanted to end his life. His plan was to drive off a cliff. When he at last pulled off the road to initiate the act, for reasons he could not explain, he turned his radio on. As he did, "I Chose You" had just started. Against a soft piano, he heard a man's voice saying:

Now, this is what the Lord says,
he who created you,
he who formed you.
"Fear not, for I have redeemed you;
I have summoned you by name; you are mine.
When you pass through the waters,
I will be with you;
when you pass through the rivers,
they will not sweep over you.
When you walk through the fire,
you will not be burned;
the flames will not set you ablaze.
For I am the LORD your God . . .
You are precious, honored in my sight . . .
and because I love you."

Isaiah 43:1–4 (as recorded on "I Chose You,"
from *More Hope* by David Teems)

The man thought God was speaking to him directly "over the airwaves," as he explained later. He did not even know it was Scripture. Even so, after a few more lines, he broke down and wept himself clean, allowing the words to wash over him, taking with them the pain that had driven his desperation.

> Do not be afraid. I am with you.
> Do not be discouraged.
> Do not be terrified.
> You did not choose me. But I chose you.
> And I will be with you always, even to the end of the age . . .
> **Select passages from Joshua 1:9; John 14:27; 15:16 (as recorded on "I Chose You," from *More Hope* by David Teems)**

At the end of the selection, another voice spoke. "That was 'I Chose You' from *More Hope* by David Teems." Realizing it was a radio broadcast, the man drove until he found a phone. He called the station and spoke to the host of *Still Waters*, Melissa Smith, and told her what had just happened. She invited him to the station, at which point she talked with him and prayed with him. Before leaving the station, she gave him a copy of David's recording.

The point is, how did one thing lead to another, then to another and to another? David is a poet. He has an ear for the music of language, something that he loves, something handed down to him by his ancestors. If he was going to serve God in any capacity, therefore, it would naturally lean toward language, toward the music and poetic movement of the Scriptures, long before Janie, or the man of the cliffs (or I) ever showed up at his door. Each miracle has miles and miles of time behind it.

ON HIS TERMS

I have struggled with depression off and on throughout my life. I get so caught up in myself and what *is not* going right that I continually miss out on what *is* going right. There are so many moments in my life when I have not seen or felt his presence, which caused me to miss and lose out on the blessings I had been given. As if we are to trust what we feel and see and think and believe at all times. It doesn't work that way. To set the record straight and not to mislead: If I have not seen or felt his presence on occasion, it is not because of *his* absence, it is because of mine. He was there. I was too distracted to notice.

The economy of God's gifts to us operates much like him who made them, who set them in motion. Like him, they have this *I will be what I will be* quality about them. You can't make them happen. You can't make them *not* happen. You can only watch and see what *does* happen. Your faith is continually being challenged, and if you think you have it all figured out, trust me, you are going to learn in a way you may not be prepared for. And then some.

> And the Lord said, "If you had faith like a grain of mustard seed, you could say to this mulberry tree, 'Be uprooted and planted in the sea,' and it would obey you."
>
> **Luke 17:6**

Faith is not denying reality. It is not pretending you don't have a problem. It is not refining the art of wearing rose-colored glasses. Faith is facing the facts, both good and bad, without being disheartened by them—and all on *his* terms. Let me repeat that: on *his* terms. The best any of us can do is to study what those terms are. Be flexible. Be nimble. Most of all, be vigilant. To live and move and have your being in him is to know not just *when* he moves but *how*. That makes us perpetual students. I am still arriving, still on my way. I am going to do my best to enjoy every miracle on that path, to learn to recognize them, to know the difference between the counterfeit and the authentic, and so on. That gives me a share in the great *I will be what I will be*. And I am grateful for that.

WATER INTO WINE

Adam James, Michael Jarrett, David MacKechnie, Kent Maxson

Whenever I get lonely

And shadows fill my head

Nothin' out there is going right

And more trouble's up ahead

All at once He's there beside me saying,

"It's gonna turn out fine"

There He goes again

Turning water into wine

CHORUS

Time and time again turning water into wine

Turning mountains into hills that I can climb

Turning darkness into light, turning wrong turns into right

He's always there turning water into wine

Yesterday the sky turned dark

And every cloud had rain

I knew the sun was gone forever

And wouldn't be back again

He just laughed and told me, "Son,

Tomorrow it will shine"

There He went again

Turning water into wine

CHORUS

Time and time again turning water into wine

Turning mountains into hills that I can climb

Turning darkness into light, turning wrong turns into right

He's always there turning water into wine

BRIDGE

Like the sun on the horizon whose colors blaze across the sky

He's the start of each new day and the last light of the night

CHORUS

Time and time again turning water into wine

Turning mountains into hills that I can climb

Turning darkness into light, turning wrong turns into right

He's always there turning water into wine

Chapter 12
I Could Grow Old Like This

The moon's being pushed by a soft autumn breeze
One look in her eyes and it's easy to see
That I could grow old like this

Kent Maxson and Randy Finchum,

"I Could Grow Old Like This"

When does something go from being new to being old? How many new toys do we get at Christmas that by the following year need to be replaced by another new toy? When do the clothes you just had to have go out of style and become yesterday's fashion? There is that brief period when your coveted new widget never leaves your sight, then slowly, over time, quietly, it never sees the light of day except when you're sorting out your old stuff. When I was in high school in the 1970s, the car that everyone wanted was the Datsun 280Z. I still think the body lines of this car are the sexiest of all time. I wanted one of these cars badly. I begged and pleaded with my dad to help me get one. I didn't have the money, and my dad couldn't afford to buy me one and still take care of my mom and sisters. (I personally thought we could do without my sisters, but that didn't fly very well when I brought the subject up.) Only the rich kids in my school got to own and drive one of these cars. We were not poor, but we were not rich either. So, life went on, and I drove my mom's old faded blue Chevy station wagon. This was followed up by my grandpa's hand-me-down Buick. Then came a long succession of small used car after small used car. When I got married for the first time, I had a Chrysler Laser. But child after child, that car gave way to vehicles more suitable for a family.

Not long after the second of my four daughters left home, I was browsing used cars on the internet when I saw it, my dream car, a blue 1975 Corvette Datsun 280Z. I was shocked that the price was something I could actually afford. I no longer needed a big car for the entire family to ride in. We had my wife's SUV for that. I started plotting and planning. One phone call and a test drive later, I drove off in my most treasured possession. It took me years to do it, but I finally owned a 280Z of my own.

To say I babied that car is an understatement. I washed and waxed it at least once a month. I worked for a very large electronics company at the time, so I installed a massive sound system. That car never spent a night outside: I cleaned out a special place in the garage and made sure that every night she was tucked in safely, protected from the elements and the cold night air. I was now the "big man on campus," and that car never got old to me. In the entire seven years I owned it, I never once thought of her as being old. She was always stunning and new. I would be driving her today had it not been for the divorce. Since I was moving back to Nashville, I needed a more practical vehicle. One of the saddest days of my life was the day my dream car drove off with her new owner.

Like you and me, our possessions age. They wear out. They lose their sheen, or we lose interest. They may even belong to someone else in time.

Even sadder is when relationships go through the same routine. They too can lose their sparkle. It happens. There are two ways it can go: You can let the relationship wither and die from neglect and other causes, or you can cultivate and care for it, maintain watch over it, and protect it from the elements. When I moved back to Nashville in 2014, I knew I was broken, that I needed to heal. In their literature, the church I started going to mentioned that they had a group called "DivorceCare." I didn't really have anything else to do at the time, so I gave it a try. There were enough divorced people to create such a group, so at least I wouldn't feel alone or awkward. There was no way I could have known how my decision to attend this class would change my life forever.

I was nervous when I walked into my first meeting. I had spoken by phone earlier in the week to Rich, who was leading the group. He listened to my story and then told me that the group met after the church services on Sunday nights. I almost didn't go, but in my heart I knew I didn't have much of a choice. I was confused, nervous. I tried to sneak into the room unnoticed. Rich saw me and introduced me to the group and did his best to make me feel welcome.

About fifteen minutes after the meeting started, a very attractive woman came into the room and sat at the only available seat, right next to me. She never acknowledged me or said anything. We never exchanged a word, not a single "Hello," "Hi," or anything for a whole year. Around that time, she and I were approached separately about co-leading a second DivorceCare group. When we finally spoke, the attraction was immediate. And mutual. We clicked, as they say. A month or so after that, we started dating. A little over a year after that, we were married. We have now been married for nine years.

HEAVEN MINDED

When I first started dating Cindy, I lived in a small house in a quiet area of Nashville. Many nights we would sit in my backyard on a swing, hold hands, and talk. I stopped focusing on the unattended particulars of the day and the clutter of tomorrow and allowed myself to relax in the moment, enjoying every precious ounce of it, savoring it, a thing she made easy. One night as we were looking at the moon I said, "I could grow old like this." At that moment, I knew God had provided me a partner to share the rest of my life with. She knew it too. So, with those thoughts in mind, before going any further, I want to consider a couple of passages from the wisdom books of the Bible, passages not unlike me and Cindy, with two very different temperaments and yet one heart between them.

> May your fountain be blessed, and may you rejoice in the wife of your youth.
>
> **Proverbs 5:18, NIV**

> Enjoy life with your wife, whom you love, all the days of this meaningless life that God has given you under the sun—all your meaningless days. For this is your lot in life and in your toilsome labor under the sun.
>
> **Ecclesiastes 9:9, NIV**

Not to judge Solomon too harshly, but these passages, at least on the surface, seem to clash. Both instruct you to enjoy your spouse, but while the first is full of joy, promise, and positivity, the second is a buzzkill. 'Meaningless! Meaningless!', says the Teacher. 'Utterly meaningless! Everything is meaningless' (Ecclesiastes 1:2, NIV). Sounds kind of tart, doesn't he? Remember, this is the guy who has to manage a household with 700 wives and almost half that many concubines. Scripture gave Adam only one wife—one, and even they had their share of struggles. But "meaningless"? We are to enjoy this "meaningless" life together? As a songwriter, word choice is vital. The same is true for books or any serious writing, and there is plenty of evidence that Solomon was a master wordsmith. The trick, therefore, of understanding this troublesome word may be in the translation, as it usually is.

The Hebrew word *hebel* [הֶבֶל], translated in the above passage as *meaningless* means "vapor or breath." Think of it as something brief, fleeting, ephemeral, as in "Charm is deceptive, and beauty is fleeting" (Proverbs 31:30, NIV)—that is, it doesn't last, it is quick lived. Other versions of the Bible translate *hebel* as "useless" or "vain." "Vanity of vanities, saith the Preacher, vanity of vanities; all is vanity" (Ecclesiastes 1:2, KJV). Without a lot of hermeneutic razzle-dazzle, let me summarize by suggesting that because life is fleeting, we should not only act accordingly, but we should do our best to be heaven-minded as well, to live and enjoy this life with the life to come in mind, making the most of it while we have it to enjoy. By doing this, the distinctions between heaven and earth fade, taking the word *meaningless* out of our vocabulary altogether. Tomorrow is promised to no one.

> Do not boast about tomorrow, for you do not know what a day may bring forth.
>
> **Proverbs 27:1, NIV**

> But about that day or hour no one knows, not even the angels in heaven, nor the Son, but only the Father.
>
> **Matthew 24:36, NIV**

SOME JUST TALK

When someone asked me once, "Why do dogs live such short life spans?" I thought of something a friend of mine once said, that it was because they get a lot of quality living done in a very short period of time. The one thing a dog understands and exercises with great energy, dedication, and bounce is unconditional love. Love is easy for them. The exercise of the gospel is easy for them. Forgiveness is easy for them. They don't waste years in learning and relearning these things. Somehow, they get it right from the beginning. Whether or not any of that is true is beside the point.

Applied to you and me, eternity is bound in the simple exercise of the gospel, whatever it asks of you—in the giving of yourself where there is need, in the joy we express in the presence of our master, and in how easy it is to forgive an offense. It is not complicated. It certainly isn't to the dog. We should envy their energy, their singularity of focus, their dedication, and their bounce. A dog provides one of the best examples of the devoted life. Their master is their life. Again, loving your neighbor is loving God. Because God is love, love has a share in eternity. Love's the stuff eternity is made of, and as mentioned earlier, eternal life doesn't begin in some remote by-and-by. It lives in the next selfless act, in the next kind word, in finding contentment at the feet of your master.

> Whoever does not love does not know God, because God is love. This is how God showed his love among us: He sent his one and only Son into the world that we might live through him. This is love: not that we loved God, but that he loved us and sent his Son as an atoning sacrifice for our sins.
>
> **1 John 4:8–10, NIV**

And he has given us this command: Anyone who loves God must also love their brother and sister.

1 John 4:21, NIV

Love brings the eternal into the temporal, timelessness into time, the supernatural into the natural. It ushers us into paradise once again, paradise here, now, present and accounted for. Love is the only way. The older I get, the more evident this becomes.

> Love, therefore, is our transport, our fare to a living Eden. Love is paradise come again. Without a complete reckoning with love, there is no reconciliation with our origins. Man without God is man without love. Man without love is not fully man; selfhood is at best imaginary.
>
> David Teems, *And Thereby Hangs a Tale:*
> *What I Really Know about the Devoted Life*
> *I Learned from My Dogs*

Though my father is no longer with us, I get glimpses of him, of his spirit, in the subtle expressions on my girls' faces, in their laughter, in the look on my mother's face when she speaks of him, and perhaps even in the movement of some of my songs. We once were all together, physically together. Then life intervened, and we were not. All that I could have said, all that I should have done, all that I neglected, and to be fair, all that I did right, to show him I love him—all these things are now memories, a record kept in my heart of hearts, in the deeper reserves. Though I am imperfect, love is perfect, and love never fails.

I have made my livelihood on songs I have conceived and put to paper. When I think about the apostle John or the apostle Paul, I think they are not mere chroniclers, men who followed Jesus and just wrote down what he said or by epiphany gave speech to what they saw and felt. There is more to it than that. We don't necessarily think of Paul as a poet, but that is what he was—our poet-prophet-evangelist-apostle Paul. Only someone with strong poetic instincts could write lines like, "If I speak in the tongues of men and angels, but have not love" (1 Corinthians 13:1) or "I want to know Christ—yes, to know the power of his resurrection and participation in his sufferings" (Philippians 3:10, NIV), or "Now the Lord is the Spirit, and where the Spirit of the Lord is, there is freedom" (2 Corinthians 3:17), and a thousand other lines rich in the life and music of heaven. Each word is inspired (breathed in), swept up not only in beautiful poetry but living poetry, eternal, written by a poet under the influence of the Almighty. We love to quote them, memorize them, even as we attempt to live them, exercise them, cultivate them, and keep them alive in our hearts.

Notice too, that in many passages, 1 Corinthians 13 among them, Paul did not include one Christian marker, that is, he did not include words like *Lord*, or *Jesus, Holy Spirit*, and so on, as most of the Scriptures do. His words are addressed to a Christian audience but also to those who are strangers to the gospel, unaccustomed to Christian vernacular. This may be an important distinction for a post-Christian America. Christians are quick to utter Scriptures and yet they back up those Scriptures with little— if anything at all. American culture is no longer persuaded by it. Indeed, there is a strong antagonism against it. And perhaps for good reasons.

Years ago, the movie *Geronimo* (1993) came out, featuring Wes Studi as Geronimo. There was one scene, one line of dialogue in particular, that got my attention, making it hard to forget. Geronimo has surrendered to the US Army and is standing under a tent with the lieutenant to whom he surrendered. During their conversation, the subject of medicine men (tribal holy men) comes up. The lieutenant asks Geronimo about them, and Geronimo says, "Some have the power. Some just talk."

We are great at pounding pulpits, at singing our songs, at breaking down the Scripture to its minute particulars as if it were some exercise of literary criticism. We quote it for impact and expect it to do all the work. But without the exercise of love, the sacrificial kind, it is all meaningless, vain, a mere breath, as Solomon said. More plainly, it is hot air. Without love, without humility and right thinking, Scripture is not only impotent, but its use can harden something in the heart. That is a strange pill to swallow, but I think we have all witnessed those who began well, railed loudly and convincingly, but ended poorly.

God wants us to enjoy this journey. He designed it for our growth, health, wonder, and felicity. We often perceive God as an old, white-bearded fuddy-duddy who doesn't want us to have any fun. We forget that he created all the beauty that we behold, that he did it for you and for me. He made both man and woman, with all their complementary parts—physically and emotionally. Because the world we know is a sinful world, it may seem, impossible to imagine that it was created as perfect. But it was. God anticipated perfection in man, in you and in me. We were designed for perfection and to understand perfection. And even now, this far downstream that same perfection is still within our reach. Whether you're with the wife or husband "of your youth" or if you are single, you are invited to share in the perfection of God through Christ. Think of the possibilities.

OLD LIKE THIS

Randy Finchum, Kent Maxson

Her head on my shoulder as we sit on the swing
Like a tune on a fiddle she plays my heart strings
The moon's being pushed by a soft autumn breeze
One look in her eyes, it's easy to see
That I could grow old like this

Marshmallows roasting, a silhouette by the fire
The last glass of wine before we retire
The embers are glowing, there's a chill in the air
Holding her hand, stroking her hair
Yeah, I could grow old like this

> **CHORUS**
>
> I've looked around for so many years
> Could it be this simple? Is this what love is?
> I only know how I feel
> And I've never been so content
> Yeah, I could grow old like this

We pull back the covers and climb into bed
Thank God for each other as we say our prayers
I'm lost in the moment and finally at peace
She lays in my arms and we fall asleep
Yeah, I could grow old like this

No Way Out But Through

CHORUS

I've looked around for so many years

Could it be this simple? Is this what love is?

I only know how I feel

I've never been so content

Yeah, I could grow old like this

Chapter 13
Memories, Not Dreams

Yet you do not know what tomorrow will bring. What is your life?
For you are a mist that appears for a little time and then vanishes.

James 4:14

When I was in grade school I thought people in high school were old. When I got to high school, people in college were old. As I neared the end of college, it became evident that the next stage in life was adulthood, which meant a job, a car note, a house mortgage, and other grown-up stuff. Some of my friends who had married young were having kids. In my mind, when you reached this stage, it meant you were officially over the hill, because my friends could no longer hang out whenever they wanted to.

When I got married the first time, my wife had two young daughters. I skipped the whole young married couple stage and jumped right into being a dad whose life revolved around providing for a family. Life became more about providing than about being dad. Or it seems that way to me now. In the house I grew up in, one of the biggest sins you could commit was not being responsible. I have already mentioned being kicked out of college. I had always known *how* to be responsible and what that meant. Putting it into practice, however, was another story. Getting married changed all that. I had little choice but to become responsible, and it was time.

My parents were now grandparents and senior citizens, so in my mind they had transitioned from old to ancient. Time zoomed by and before I knew it the youngest of my children was finishing college. It was about that time my wife informed me that she wanted a divorce—so much for growing old with the wife of my youth. I had always imagined that growing old included a wife. That was part of the deal if you were a good and responsible person. Then all too soon I had to face navigating old age by myself.

In this final chapter I must retell some of the darker moments of my story to clarify the point I wish to make: No matter how dark the way, how hopeless, or how impossible the odds, there is a way out. And if there is hope for me, there is hope for you.

When my divorce was final, I had no road map. I felt abandoned, lost. As I played out my future in my mind, it got dark quick. I was convinced that sometime down the road someone would notice I hadn't shown up for church, or for another Al-Anon meeting. They would stop by my house and find me slumped over in my easy chair, cold as a stone. I convinced myself that my life was drawing to a close, that I would die alone. It was certainly not the way I thought my life would play out when I was young, if I thought about it at all.

I had several choices to make when I moved back to Nashville. Maybe it is a product of age, desperation, or some measure of both, but it occurred to me in a rare moment of clarity that I could either get bitter or get better. Forgive the cliché, but what had once been important to me no longer seemed to matter. Somehow I had become "old." A playback of my life revealed a sad and continuing series of demanding moments, those immediate take-care-of-it-now events—so much so that I seemed to miss the journey altogether. It was like driving from Dallas to Lubbock and remembering only the blacktop highway, and none of the trees, cacti, sand (there was lots of sand), buildings, or towns. It was unsettling to realize there were more miles behind me than there were ahead.

I made the decision at last to slow down. I was determined that life was no longer going to be one big race down some metaphorical highway. I was going to see some scenery. I was going to live me some life. Not only was I going to remember the journey, I was going to do my best to make it memorable, to salvage what I could and rethink the way I had always done things. When I did that, something marvelous happened.

ANOTHER CHANCE AT LIFE

From our earliest moments together, I realized to my deepest joy that Cindy was the person I wanted to spend the rest of my life with, the one I wanted to create memories with—new memories, better memories, redemptive memories—happy, life-altering, and life-enhancing, the kind of memories that bring a kind of mysticism back to life, an elevated life, the kind God had in mind from the beginning. I was tuned to each moment as I passed through each one of them, life becoming more about the journey than the destination. The simple things we did together were all I wanted to do until the day God would take me from this planet.

Between God and Cindy, I was given another chance at life. Because of that, I wanted to stay present *in* that life, to live fully in the time remaining to me. Among the many things we talked about were those things we had never done that we had always wanted to do. There were things I denied myself in the past, things I might have done but didn't for the fear gnawing away at my faith—fear of failure, fear of success, fear of the unknown. Anyone who knows Cindy knows she fears nothing, that she thrives on new experiences, new adventures, that they seem to seek her out. She does not fear living life on the edge. Perhaps Captain Kirk had someone like Cindy in mind when he said, "To boldly go." It is no exaggeration to say she has helped me to reassess my faith, to reassess my belief in my own gifts that I might pursue, dream, and do things I may never have attempted before. And fearlessly, too. Cindy has the kind of spiritual backbone that cannot help but rub off on me.

> Now faith is confidence in what we hope for and assurance about what we do not see.
>
> **Hebrews 11:1, NIV**

It has been my habit, as I said earlier, to worry about everything—every bill that is due, every task that has to be completed or has been ignored, every responsibility that has to be met. If I am not worrying, then I worry that I am not worrying, that I have forgotten something I should be worrying about. It has been difficult to admit that to worry, especially in so chronic and consistent a manner, is contrary to the wisdom of Scripture. Worry is the great underminer, the great saboteur of our peace and our ability to accomplish what has been assigned to us by divine appointment.

> Therefore do not worry about tomorrow, for tomorrow will worry about itself. Each day has enough trouble of its own.
>
> **Matthew 6:34, NIV**

If I struggle with faith, and I do, I suspect I am not alone. In a culture that has so many distractions—a scrolling, swiping culture, a social media-addicted culture, one that keeps our attention jumping from one shiny object to the next, from one spectacle, one "influencer" to the next, on and on and on and on until hours have passed and your brain becomes like a flat tire—it is easy to fatigue faith to the point of deflation and immobility. Somewhere along the way I started confusing *responsibility* with *response ability*, which are two different things. I can spend endless hours putting out fires and responding to every major and minor event that begs my attention. Or I can learn (or relearn) to live responsibly, to not only find equilibrium but to honor it, follow it, and cultivate it in my life—that balance that helps me prioritize my life with wisdom. If Scripture has anything to add here, it might be "When I was a child, I spoke like a child, I thought like a child, I reasoned like a child. When I became a man, I gave up childish ways" (1 Corinthians 13:11).

Control of any situation rests ultimately in God's capable hands, but I can find that point of cooperation between him and me. Do I have faith in God, or in the stressful moment do I abandon him and trust in my own wisdom and devices? I do not want to be a casual observer of life, but one who is actively engaged—a participant in the marvelous experiences God brings into my life. The more I share his likeness, the more likely I am to know his mind and how he wants me to choose and to act.

Cindy and I often talk about not knowing how much time we have left and how we want no regrets. One day it came to me: "I want to die with memories, not dreams." I went on a songwriting retreat and shared this line with a couple of my associates, Adam James Deiboldt and Alyssa Trahan. We were writing in my room, so Cindy was in the background. She would throw out the occasional thumbs up or thumbs down as we worked, which helped to keep us on track. There are reasons I love all my songs, but this one felt special. It captures the deeper parts of what I feel as I travel through these latter stages of my life. To know it was inspired by Cindy makes it that much more special, and my gratitude even sweeter.

As we turn to the last pages of this book, I have included the lyric of "Memories, Not Dreams." And that is the best we can do—make memories, glorious ones, simple, full of life, full of the moment. Eternity is now. Love is now. With life whizzing by at the velocity it does, it is easy to miss these events. Accelerated speed is the rule these days, not the exception. Therefore, live the exceptional. Find your own tempo. It's there. It's been there underneath the noise all along—your own rhythm, the meter and language of your own song. Some of you may be thinking, "What a mess this guy has made of his life, what can he tell me?" And I would be the first to say you are right. But every day is a new start.

I hope by now you understand that I am in recovery, that I have learned a few things and that there is so much more to learn. The point is if there is hope for me, there is hope for you. For all the messes I have made, all the things I neglected to do or refused to live up to, the light came on at last. It was bright, at times dazzling, but it opened my eyes. It took some getting used to in the beginning, but my eyes adjusted quickly, and I am grateful for it.

There is nothing more terrifying than to get close to the end of the road with a dream left unsatisfied, if it begins to fade or seem like a cruel joke, like you sat in on a game for which you were unprepared, or you feel guilty for not doing the things necessary to make some dream a reality, and life has become one long protracted punishment, one we inflict on ourselves. That is one long sentence, but the punishment we inflict on ourselves is also one long sentence. Dreams are natural, even necessary. Without them, I think we are a little less human. We may, as grown-ups, think of them as goals or aspirations, those things that drive us, that move our ambitions further. The best dreams are the ones inspired by God. Beacon-like, they are a light in a dark place to keep us on course. They tend to have our spiritual, emotional, and cognitive DNA about them, our shapes and personhood. They are a part of who we are, how we negotiate life, how we stay afloat when waters rise. If we pray for wisdom and discernment, we can know the difference between the inspired dreams and the more deceptive ones that do not honestly reflect who we are in and before God.

I suppose the lyric of this song becomes a cautionary tale, a warning of a kind that may show you there is something better—especially those of you who struggle with getting older or feel that life has not gone the way you once thought it should. The good news is, there is a way of seeing and perceiving that can literally "change your mind," that will salvage the life you feel has slipped away from you, that can put a dream, a real sweet one, in its place, giving you the desire, the energy, and courage to pursue it. It is about creating memories, those very real things we have collected over the years and are still creating every day—even those that made you hurt, those against which you struggled to survive (and did!). Those are worthy of us as well. Either way, I hope this lyric, like the pages you've just read, provides enough light for you to see or detect the next step, then the step after that, and the step after that—that it may illumine the most prized thoughts of a most prized and desired life, one that remains reachable and doable, whatever your age.

MEMORIES, NOT DREAMS

Adam James Deiboldt, Kent Maxson, Alyssa Trahan

It's been written on pages and stone
But it's just words until it hits home
Life is shorter than you think
And the truth is another day is never guaranteed

You're born and suddenly you're sixteen
The next morning you wake up at 53
Those one-day someday plans you had
They never came to life, you say you never had the chance

> **CHORUS**
> Everybody's time is gonna come
> That's the one thing we can all count on
> I don't know when it will be, but when it's my time to leave
> I wanna die with memories, not dreams

I don't know how much time I have left
But I know I don't want to have any regrets
Work and bills and income taxes, life fills up with these
    distractions
Before you know it you're looking back and wondering what
    happened

> **CHORUS**
> Everybody's time is gonna come
> That's the one thing we can all count on

I don't know when it will be, but when it's my time to leave

I wanna die with memories, not dreams

BRIDGE

I'm gonna take that trip, and call that friend,

Tell the ones I love, I love 'em again.

Do all things I always said

And maybe a few I didn't yet

About the Authors

Kent Maxson is an award-winning Nashville songwriter whose songs have been performed on international TV and radio. "From Where I'm Sitting," cowritten with Garth Brooks, earned Kent a gold record. Originally from Midland, Texas, Kent now lives in Nashville with his wife, Cindy.

More at: www.kentmaxson.com

David Teems is a best-selling author of *Majestie: The King Behind the King James Bible* (Thomas Nelson/Harper Collins) and *Tyndale: The Man Who Gave God an English Voice* (Thomas Nelson/Harper Collins). David lives with his wife, Benita, in Nashville.

More at: www.davidteems.com

Scan QR Code for access to Kent's music.

www.ingramcontent.com/pod-product-compliance
Lightning Source LLC
Chambersburg PA
CBHW021148130626
46554CB00005B/1719

* 9 7 9 8 9 8 7 1 3 1 4 9 7 *